IMAGES

of America

ZEPHYRHILLS

ON THE COVER: Summy's Cottage in 1912 festively hosted the Grand Army of the Republic (GAR) Encampment. The local cornet band was in attendance. Summy's Cottage was located at Fifth Avenue and Eighth Street, abutting Neukom's Drug Store, and was later known as Boggs House and Bolt Apartments. The GAR was a fraternal organization composed of veterans of the Union army who had served in the American Civil War. They held annual encampments from 1866 to 1949. It was a strong special interest group in political movements. The cover photograph is provided by Rick Moore, historian and collector, who is a keen preserver of local history. (Courtesy of Rick Moore.)

IMAGES
of America

ZEPHYRHILLS

Madonna Jervis Wise

ARCADIA
PUBLISHING

Published by Arcadia Publishing
Charleston SC, Chicago IL, Portsmouth NH, San Francisco CA

Library of Congress Control Number: 2009933696

For all general information contact Arcadia Publishing at:
Telephone 843-853-2070
Fax 843-853-0044
E-mail sales@arcadiapublishing.com
For customer service and orders:
Toll-Free 1-888-313-2665

Visit us on the Internet at www.arcadiapublishing.com

This book is dedicated to three unique individuals who happen to be my children: J. Jervis Wise, Mamie V. Jervis Wise, and Rachel Beth Jervis Wise—you are my life's inspiration!

CONTENTS

ACKNOWLEDGMENTS

Synergy is the combined action of two or more entities to produce a greater sum than the single worker individually. We problem solve and experience more effectively as collaborators. With that said, I have many to thank for this book, *Zephyrhills*. I wish to acknowledge Jeff Miller, Clereen Morrill Brunty, Rick Moore, Caroline Marlette, Carolyn Falls, Irene Dobson, Margaret Seppanen, Nancy Massey Perkins, Genevieve Smith, Linda Sante, Nick Linville, and Victoria Reeves for their contributions, assistance, and kind guidance. My husband, Ernest Wise, media specialist and educator, provided invaluable resources, assistance, encouragement, and consultation.

Kudos to the Zephyrhills Historical Society, the Depot Museum, the Pioneer Florida Museum, the West Pasco Historical Association, Zephyrhills Main Street, Inc., and the Zephyrhills High School (ZHS) 100 ad hoc task force for their preservation of historical treasures and memories.

INTRODUCTION

The town of Zephyrhills was formally established in 1910 and celebrates its 100th anniversary at the March 2010 Founder's Day Parade, a cherished annual tradition. The history however, is much broader than the 1910–2010 span. Native Americans were the first to occupy the area. Unfortunately we do not have records of their leaders, institutions, and ways of life but have surmised through anthropologists and historians that these first inhabitants were hunters and gatherers. Zephyrhills was a prime location for the Native Americans, who needed a clean and ample water supply, stone for tools, and plentiful firewood. They lived in villages in the area, particularly around Lake Buddy and Lake Zephyr. Remnants and artifacts from the area, now housed in the local museums, have provided clues to their day-to-day life.

The first recorded history began with the arrival of European explorers, such as Ponce de Leon in 1513 and De Soto in 1539. The area was under Spanish and some French influence until 1763, when Great Britain gained control of Florida. As an indirect consequence of the American Revolution regarding allies, Spain obtained a second era of control, which was short-lived. British influence on the continent was quite established by this time, and Spain soon ceded Florida to the United States in 1821. Florida became a state in 1845. In the late 19th century, agriculture took hold when cattle ranching and settlers began appearing in the area, particularly close to streams and lakes.

The Oakdale community near present-day Zephyrhills was the first settlement with residences, a school, and a post office. Thus the modern story unfolds.

Simon J. Temple, who had many business dealings throughout Florida, purchased 280 acres on November 11, 1886, for $1,026.69 from Florida Railway and Navigation Corporation. Temple named the area Abbott after Dr. Joseph M. Abbott. The original plat of the town was laid out and recorded on April 18, 1888. When the train came through in 1896, "Station" was affixed to the town's name of Abbott. Abbott was abundant with virgin pine, which would later serve as a source and origin for employment when lumber, turpentine, and blasting powder companies evolved. Citrus and agrarian industries thrived for many years in the area as well. A voting district was established in 1893 and a post office in 1896.

Next, a Civil War veteran from Pennsylvania, Capt. Howard B. Jeffries, purchased land in 1909 to initiate a settlement for other Yankee Civil War veterans. The official tourist book from the time reported that 5 acres cost $50. Jeffries was said to have been traveling through the area and stopped at one of the more scenic locations, LeHeup Hill, where he gazed down on rolling hills and felt zephyr-like breezes. He renamed the area that had been Oakdale and later Abbott as Zephyrhills. The town was incorporated in 1914.

From those early roots, the region grew and developed with some essential ongoing themes that linger yet today. Throughout the 1920s and 1930s, the locale was agrarian with one major industry, Greer's Lumber Mill. Farming remained the base of the economy throughout the 1920s and 1930s. The Great Depression hit Zephyrhills hard—the only bank in town closed, as did Greer's Mill. Lumbering continued as a theme, however; when I. A. Krusen arrived in 1932, he developed Krusen Land and Timber Company. Walter Gall bought 30,000 acres for $3 per acre and also lumbered, then he resold it (the area including what is now Saddlebrook). Gall was also instrumental in the building of Highway 54 in 1936 as a major thoroughfare right through town from his position on the state road department. In addition, he was personnel director for the Works Progress Administration (WPA) during the Great Depression and recruited thousands of men back to work. His additional business was the Gall Silica Sand Mine in neighboring Polk County.

Numerous service industries from the 1940s forward then began to emerge. Emil Reutimann, for example, established a thriving automobile sales and repair shop. A new industry, Hercules Powder Plant, was opened in 1946 and provided jobs for the area. The airport was built in 1942 as training ground for the Army Air Force. A Kentucky dairy farmer, Jack Linville, relocated here in 1952 and would make agricultural history with his innovative poultry farming practices, which included producing his own feed source for the chickens. Don Robinson emerged in 1961 with the establishment of a business, Zephyrhills Water Company, which would become an iconic local symbol.

The 1950s brought a significant and steady influx of seasonal folks who established an increasingly stronger service-industry identity to accommodate the seasonal visitors. Present-day Zephyrhills emerged in the 1950s and 1960s. The physical shape of the town as it is in the 21st century unfolded in these decades.

Throughout Zephyrhills's history, there was migration. It is somewhat rare today to find citizens who were born in Florida or who have more than one or two generations of family in the area. Nearly everyone has a tale of relocation—be it their own or their family's. With this adventurous pioneer spirit so abundant, Zephyrhills has readily accepted newcomers over time. Perhaps the origin of the title "Friendly City" comes from this heritage of openness and acceptance. The area has also produced many innovators and thinkers. Walter Gall, I. A. Krusen, Emil Reutimann, Willa Rice, and many more overcame barriers, worked hard, and produced results.

One

CENTENNIAL CELEBRATION

The centennial celebration of Zephyrhills occurs in 2010. Roberto Escobar of Main Street, Inc., designed the official brand for the city's centennial. The committee that organized the event consisted of chair Tim Urban, vice chair Clereen Morrill Brunty, secretary Madonna Jervis Wise, and treasurer Ron Cherry. Members included Jud Baggett, Tracey St. Onge Barnes, Elaine McKendree Benjamin, Chris Black, Clyde Bracknell, Dave Camper, Cyndi Craig, Ann Crawford, Irene Dobson, Greg First, Luan Gore, Mary Lee Going Griffith, Betty Hall, Gary Hatrick, Gregg Hilferding, Louie Holt, Betty Jo Turner Hyder, Louise Lashley, Caroline Marlette, Melanie Massey Foltz, Christi Spoto Mastrogianikis, Craig Milburn, Barbara Peeples Miller, Glenn Miller, Barbara Bales Moore, Jean Nathe, Anne Brooke Neukom, George Neukom Jr., Judy Norris, Gerri Painter, Nancy Massey Perkins, Sandy Pricher, Ginger Potwin Rutan, Margaret Seppanen, Eddie Smith, Lance Smith, Tracy Snyder, Steve Spina, Maria Spoto-Ray, Mark Steve, Clayton Stokes, Lenora Pollock Stokes, Terry Turner, Steve Van Gorden, and Brenda Welcher. (Courtesy of Roberto Escobar and Zephyrhills Main Street, Inc.)

Driving into Zephyrhills on Highway 54 in 1956 provided a panoramic view including pasture land, residences, trailer camps, and businesses. As one entered the city limits, a gaze to the right allowed a view of Zephyr Lake, which once hosted the "tin can tourists" of the 1930s and beyond. (Courtesy of Florida Library and Archives, Florida Department of State.)

Zephyrhills between 1910 and 1920 had residences on Eighth Avenue (Fifth Avenue in the postcard). Oxen were preferred to horses because of the rigorous sand turf. Cattle gaps were in place on the west, north, and south entrances to the city limits. These prevented cattle from coming into the city from the open ranges. A few folks still had a horse and wagon for conveyance; a gate had to be provided parallel to the rails, because the horses could not gain footing on the slick rails. (Courtesy of Florida Library and Archives, Florida Department of State.)

10

The livery stable in Zephyrhills was essential before automobiles were abundant and provided a place to rent or board a horse within walking distance of hotel or home. Tillie Reutimann Smith remembered when one could rent a "surry with a fringe on top" at the local livery, Edmondson's. (Courtesy of Zephyrhills Depot Museum–Zephyrhills Historical Association [ZHA].)

Zephyrhills in 1919 was vastly rural. Homes and lots within the town were fenced, because cattle as well as hogs roamed free. Each house had a chicken yard, cow, garden, and citrus for sustainability. (Courtesy of West Pasco Historical Society [WPHS].)

The GAR building was constructed in 1911 by Civil War veterans. Heart-pine lumber from Greer's Mill was hauled by oxen cart for its construction. The hall featured an auditorium, concert hall, movie house, and meeting place. (Courtesy of *Zephyrhills News* [ZN].)

Geiger's Mercantile Store on Gall Boulevard was operated by James Geiger, known affectionately as "Uncle Jim." He also served as a city councilman and later postmaster. John Geiger, patriarch of the local Geiger family, came from Ocala just after the Civil War and purchased land from Simon Temple. (Courtesy of ZHA.)

The interior of Geiger's Mercantile revealed the wares of the day. Samuel E. Nyce wrote in the November 23, 1911, *Zephyrhills Colonist* of his arrival to Zephyrhills: "In most every direction, the saw and hammer were heard, mostly by amateurs. Geiger's Store, Orcutt's Barber Shop, the Zephyrhills Inn, Mr. Summy's house . . . these places had, Phoenix-like-arisen, the black oaks were disappearing and general industry appeared to be on." (Courtesy of ZHA.)

The history of Zephyrhills is full of picnics at Crystal Springs. Angie Geiger LeHeup, local 1929 graduate, said the first-ever alumni reunion was held there. The location was used by families and every group in town for recreation—a marvelous picnic and a swim in the remarkable springs. The area of Crystal Springs was founded in 1911 as a socialist endeavor with joint ownership of property for what was coined "the common good society." The springs attracted a socialist group from the north who settled in Ruskin as well as Crystal Springs. Their goal was to raise vegetables in a cooperative; however, by the 1920s, the socialist experiment was abandoned. (Courtesy of Florida Library and Archives, Florida Department of State.)

The Zephyrhills Cornet Band, which later became the Citizen Band, was a frequent parade participant throughout the state. Legend has it that at the October 24, 1910, event in which the Circuit Court of Pasco County gave the Colony Company clear title to land, people descended upon the company to find out which parcels of land were theirs. Harold S. Skogstad said things were "getting out of hand" and decided his friends should grab their horns and drums to generate some music and calm the crowd. The band was well-liked, and the Cornet Band was born. Without uniforms for two years, their first uniforms were white shirts, pants, and caps. (Courtesy of ZHA.)

Chancey family members were early settlers to the area and often transported visitors by oxen cart to view the 5-acre tracts of land plotted out by the Colony Company. In 1910, the 5-acre plots sold for $50, which included a lot in town and stock in the company. The Chancey brothers were known for their well-trained oxen teams that performed numerous other tasks, such as supplying telephone poles for the growing Tampa Electric Company and delivering cordwood to the racks of the railroad depot for the locomotives. From left to right are Cordelia (standing in the wagon), Jeff, Bessie, Lubelle, Sara Frances, Abner "Abe," Louis "Luke," Jess, and John. (Courtesy of ZHA.)

14

The Zephyrhills Hotel was built in 1917. It was the site for formal events. Coverage of the Junior-Senior Banquet of May 15, 1919, reported, "Hotel dining room was decorated with class colors and two large American flags stood in place of Lyle Gilbert and Dale Leonard, members of the senior class who were fighting in France [in World War I]. A three course dinner was served in an inviting style. The evening was spent in passing jokes and conundrums." The hotel was torn down in 1971. (Courtesy of ZHA.)

The Seaboard Airline Depot was an important feature built in 1896. The Seaboard Railroad passed through Abbott in 1896 with a stop in a town, Herndon, to the north. (Courtesy of ZHA.)

The railroad was a wonderful linkage for the community. African American workers were instrumental in the construction of the rail tracks. The Atlantic Coast Line Railroad Depot on South Avenue was built in 1927. B. F. Parsons, Zephyrhills mayor, was the station agent for two decades. It featured four passenger train stops daily. The building had wide overhangs, exterior platforms, and segregated waiting rooms with areas for passenger travel and shipping. It was closed in 1970, moved to the present site at the Depot Park in 1987, and currently houses the Zephyrhills Depot Museum. (Courtesy of ZHA.)

Helen Miller poses with a parasol at the park in 1924. A dedicated member of the Tourist Club, she energetically pepped up many evenings with dancing and giving dance lessons at the Legion Hall. Honored as 1965 Citizen of the Year, she also created a group, Merriel Miller Dancers. (Courtesy of ZHA.)

By the end of 1912, the population of Zephyrhills was more than 1,500. The 20th century brought progress that began transforming an agricultural town to a tourism and retirement community. This photograph depicts the Model Ts as they traverse the terrain on the streets of early Zephyrhills. The Model T, also known as the Tin Lizzie, was first produced about 1908 and was generally recognized as the first affordable automobile. Imagine driving a Model T down the streets of Zephyrhills; one can almost hear the high-pitched horn sounding. (Courtesy of Ernest Wise.)

Emil Reutimann Sr. operated the first garage on Highway 301 at Third Avenue. Emil and Amalie Reutimann moved to Zephyrhills in 1915 via Tampa from Switzerland. "Zephyrhills was just a place out in the country with streets of sand. I can remember Hennington's Department and Grocery Store [Mrs. Hennington had the department store and her son had the grocery store] and Penry's Department Store," said their daughter, Tillie. At first, Emil Reutimann went to work for Jim Greer doing machinist work on his sawmill, which was located on Wire Road. He then opened a small garage, which turned into a larger garage on Highway 301, and his wife, Amalie, worked as the bookkeeper. (Courtesy of the Reutimann family.)

The south entrance columns to Zephyrhills in the 1920s were one of two welcoming visitors into the city proper. The Zephyrhills Colony Company was concerned with rural colonists as well as townsfolk. Farmers participated in social, religious, and civic development of the city. To the official town's slogan of "The City of Pure Water," locals added "Friendly City" because of the warmth shown in the community. (Courtesy of Florida Library and Archives, Florida Department of State.)

Zephyrhills Main Street in 1910 was thriving. There was a continual evolution in regard to the city's name. The area was first known as Oakdale, then Abbott, then Hegman, and back to Abbott Station. By 1910, the Zephyrhills Colony Company was organized to purchase, advertise, and sell Zephyrhills land to all veterans throughout the North. The plot of Zephyrhills followed generally that of the Abbott plot of 1888. (Courtesy of Rick Moore and Florida Library and Archives, Florida Department of State.)

18

ZEPHYRHILLS, FLA.

They were known as "tin can tourists" in 1910. From the colony's inception, Zephyrhills attracted seasonal tourists to the area. Several times over the years, Robert Nichols, a resident and teacher, mentioned Zephyrhills. He later discovered that his father visited Zephyr Park, where he and his parents camped on their trip to St. Petersburg to find work. They pulled a small wooden trailer behind their car in which they slept. Robert recalled that while they were camping by the beautiful lake, a citrus truck pulled up to the campground and dumped a huge load of oranges. He said he had never tasted an orange that good before. He said that ever since his visit to Zephyrhills and Lake Zephyr, he had wondered if it was still the small and friendly town that he had remembered from the 1930s. Canning in tin was quite the innovation in the early 1900s. The tin can never completely replaced glass jars for canning at home. The cans were put together by a tin smith. (Caption and photograph courtesy of Lynn Nichols Timmons.)

Andrean "A. D." and Frances E. Penry built a department store on East Seventh Street just across from their chief competitor, Hennington's (Hennington's was the third store to open in the colony). Penry was manager of the Zephyrhills Colony's first baseball team and a real child advocate. Later his daughter, Addie Craig, and her children were active members of the Welfare League, which became the Women's Civic League and evolved into the Women's Club. This 1910 photograph shows Charlie Boggs (left) and A. D. Penry in front of Penry's Store. (Courtesy of ZN.)

The "Grand Stand," which was located where the Chamber of Commerce Building was later placed, was a gathering place for events. Notice the sidewalk, which was the very first to be built in Zephyrhills. The photograph displays the tall telegraph poles (a major source of communication), businesses, and the depot in the background. (Courtesy of Rick Moore.)

A view from the train traveling through Zephyrhills in 1910 provided a panorama. Trains were significant to the early industries, including lumber and turpentine. At a May 1979 gathering, three Zephyrhills friends—Harold Emery, former school board member and Seaboard Railroad agent; J. H. Mott; and D. A. Storms—reminisced about the many years of contributing to the quality of life in their beloved Zephyrhills. Mott, father of eight, was the Seaboard Railroad agent for many years. Storms, father of three, was a longtime businessman in Zephyrhills. All were tireless workers in the First Baptist Church, and all served at various times on the school board for Pasco County. (Courtesy of Ernest Wise.)

Parades are popular still today in Zephyrhills and had early origins. In September 1913, a parade marked the opening of the school term with banners displaying the various classes. There were 171 students enrolled in the school for that term with five teachers. (Courtesy of Bernie Wickstrom, given to Ernest Wise for the 1984 Southern Association of Colleges and Schools Accreditation [SACS] Presentation for ZHS.)

The downtown of Zephyrhills in its early days reflected the era. Highlights of the decade included women being given the right to vote by the 19th Amendment and Prohibition in 1919. The local school drama production in 1919 was entitled *Her Honor the Mayor*—a political satire on women's suffrage. (Courtesy of Ernest Wise.)

When colonists arrived, temporary tents went up throughout the area to house the visitors and prospective settlers. Construction of homes and businesses came next. Greer's Mill was operated by Jim Greer, who sold lumber to colony founder Howard Jeffries for the new construction. Greer operated a sawmill, planing mill, and turpentine still at the foot of Greer Hill. He also helped construct the Seaboard Depot. (Courtesy of Ernest Wise.)

Three year old Bearing Grove, Zephyrhills, Fla.

This advertisement of an orange grove revealed a "three year old grove bearing fruit" with a local resident showing off a plump orange. In 2009, Florida produced 70 percent of U.S. citrus (second only to Brazil in orange juice production). The citrus trees date back to the Spanish, who brought them in the 1500s and recognized that the soil and climate were conducive. With railroad transportation in the 1800s, consumer demand grew. Zephyrhills, like all of Florida, was hit by the great freeze of 1894–1895, and many groves were replanted—some migrating southward. Yet today in Zephyrhills, groves dot the landscape. (Courtesy of Rick Moore.)

Residences on 8th Ave., Zephyrhills, Fla.

Residences are shown as they appeared in Zephyrhills in the mid-1910s. George R. Pomeroy was a prominent contractor/realtor and developer in Zephyrhills. This photograph was taken while at a gathering at the Summy House, looking eastward, and it depicts a view of the streets and residences. (Courtesy of Florida Library and Archives, Florida Department of State.)

A steam locomotive train provided images while traveling through Zephyrhills in 1910. The excitement of the locomotive was wonderment, awe, and showmanship. Local literature discusses stocking the cordwood to fuel the engines, which indicates that the early locomotives were fired by wood. This was generally the universal fuel until the Civil War, at which time many were converted to coal burners and later oil. By the 1940s, diesel was used. (Courtesy of Florida Library and Archives, Florida Department of State.)

The open sand streets of early Zephyrhills were abundant with free-roaming livestock. Zephyrhills was indicative of the state of Florida, which has the longest-lasting heritage of ranching in the United States. Feuds between cattlemen and local city government in regard to the free-roaming nuisance of animals ravaging through gardens and outside businesses were ongoing, as documented in city council minutes. Cracker cattle, free range, and cattle drives were mainstays of the early decades. (Courtesy of ZHA.)

Spanish moss (also called Florida moss, long moss, and graybeard) at Zephyr Park must have been a real novelty for the Northern settlers to the area. Spanish moss was harvested for years as a stuffing material in furniture and mattresses. (Courtesy of Rick Moore.)

According to the Works Progress Administration (WPA), Zephyr Park, begun in 1937, was originally planned to cover 150 acres with a lake outlined in the shape of Florida. As shown in this photograph, it provided a place for canoeing. (Courtesy of ZHA.)

Zephyr Park in 1937 was a place of respite during the Great Depression, which impacted Zephyrhills and the daily life of its citizens. An overhead irrigation system was quite the innovation. (Courtesy of ZHA.)

The Seaboard Depot was constructed in 1896 and is still standing as the old part of the present depot. Abbott Station shipped a great deal of naval stores and timber. (Courtesy of ZHA.)

The first school located at Seventh Avenue and Sixth Street opened in 1910. It had four rooms on the first floor with a wide hall and stairway leading to the second floor. The one-room schoolhouses of Union, Childers, Wesley (located in Wesley Chapel), and Independence closed at the end of the school term of 1909–1910, and the new school opened in September 1910. (Courtesy of WPHS.)

A street scene of early Zephyrhills depicts Hotel Zephyr and surrounding businesses. Resident Andrew Wagner wrote in 1912, "Walk rite [sic] in and look around and see how you like it. You will find the door open most of the time." (Courtesy of ZHA.)

Zephyrhills in 1910 reflected the growth and change of the country. This was the first time that the United States was recognized as an industrialized country. Known as the "over there" era, the town was affected by World War I, and the historical accounts recall the many boys who served in Europe. (Courtesy of ZHA.)

Capt. Howard B. Jeffries's home in Zephyrhills was built in 1910 and had four rooms. It is still in excellent condition and currently is used as an attorney's office by Kara Hardin. It was previously occupied by Forrest Earl Hart and Steven and Eileen Herman. The location maintains most of the original features. (Courtesy of WPHS.)

The Bible Gospel Chapel was built in 1910 and is the oldest church structure in Zephyrhills. It has unique hand-crafted block. Jesse Stebbins, son of pioneer realtor A. E. Stebbins, was the first pastor. (Courtesy of Rick Moore.)

Early construction in the colony included craftsmen working on Penry's Store. It was then located on Seventh Street East. In the early decades, Seventh Street East (on what was then the east side of the railroad tracks) was considered the main thoroughfare. Later Fifth Avenue became the main street. (Courtesy of Margaret Seppanen.)

A group of local capitalists built Hotel Zephyr for approximately $25,000. For 50 years after it was opened at Thanksgiving 1912, it served as the city's primary hotel. The announcement for investors in the Zephyrhills Hotel Company stated, "This company was formed for the purpose of building and conducting a first class moderately priced hotel for three reasons: 1) the urgent need here for an up-to-date hotel; 2) the great factor such a hotel would be in the development of our Colony; and 3) the profits that would be sure to come to its stockholders." (Courtesy of ZHA.)

Neukom's Drug Store was the center of downtown Zephyrhills and was opened by Lorena Mae Leatherman Neukom ("Neukie") in 1921. It was moved to its location as depicted in the photograph in 1935. Known as a popular location with a folksy restaurant area that was a local hangout, the restaurant coined a game, Scratch—a system for deciding who would pay for the gang's coffee each morning. The drugstore closed in 2001. (Courtesy of Phyllis Geiger Debien.)

The Seaboard Air Line Railroad Depot was located between Seventh Street East (currently a one-way street running north) and Seventh Street West (now Highway 301). The Village Inn Restaurant currently sits on the location. (Courtesy of ZHA.)

The Peni-Saver Store in downtown Zephyrhills was a modern grocery store for the era. Owners included F. Earl Hart and later Wilbur Blackburn. (Courtesy of ZHA.)

A stroll in Zephyrhills reflected a town that passed through several stages, each leaving its mark on resources. The first was turpentine production as trees were tapped. The second was lumbering, and the third was development of real estate and agriculture. It was sometimes quipped that there were three Cs—cattle, citrus, and chickens—as staples of the agricultural industry. (Courtesy of WPHS.)

The area that was to become Pasco County was originally a part of Hernando County some 122 years ago, with the county seat in Brooksville. People in the southern part of the county disliked having to travel such a long distance for court and other legal business as it was a long, tiresome journey by horseback or oxcart. Those complaints sparked a drive to divide Hernando, and two Pasco leaders, Dr. Richard Bankston and Judge J. A. Handley, led the way. The name "Banner County" was proposed, but the legislators did not like the name because representatives of the each of the two counties thought his county was a "banner" county. As a compromise, the name Pasco was chosen in 1887 to honor the popular U.S. senator Samuel Pasco of Monticello. (Courtesy of Florida Library and Archives, Florida Department of State.)

Picnics were a mainstay in the local history. The local newspaper, the *Colonist*, announced the upcoming Fourth of July picnic in the June 26, 1919, issue: "To the people of Pasco County, be it known Zephyrhills is going to give you one of the old fashioned celebrations on July 4th at Zephyr Park. Big Day, Zephyrhills is going over the top as many of our soldier boys have returned to our country. We wish to give them a hearty welcome and show to the world we feel proud of our young men. There will be a smashing time from beginning to finish—songs, speeches, races, swimming contest and a champion ball game. In fact the ball will be kept rolling from 10 a.m. to 12 at night and a Cracker fish fry at noon. Come and bring a well-filled basket and have a picnic with your neighbors and friends." (Courtesy of Rick Moore.)

This photograph shows sawmill workers at Krusen Land and Timber Company in 1937. A civic leader, by 1960, I. A. Krusen had served for 20 years as chairman of the Zephyrhills School Trustees. Pasco County was divided into districts, each having three trustees. At a local 1963 graduation, Principal Charles Henderson paid tribute to Krusen, pointing out that Krusen had given diplomas to 23 of the last 24 graduating classes. (Krusen was convalescing from a heart attack he suffered the December before, and the students gave him a standing ovation.) (Courtesy of Florida Library and Archives, Florida Department of State.)

A view of a trailer camp along Highway 54 showed the tourist camp of winter visitors. Zephyrhills was one of the competing sites for the "tin can tourist" industry that began around 1919. With the warm weather and publicized good water, Zephyrhills was an enticing place. Folks built homemade camping trailers with plywood and canvas tops. By the 1930s, house trailers had become a popular way to vacation. The tin can group first organized in Tampa at DeSoto Park and called themselves "tin can tourists" in reference to the food they ate from tin cans, which they also frequently traded. Many towns recognized the economic impact from the visitors and competed for their presence with better parks and accommodation. With better roads and automobiles and eventually systems for electrical hookup, the sophistication increased. Some have said the name "tin can" evolved later into the "snowbirds" of today. (Courtesy of Florida Library and Archives, Florida Department of State.)

In 1916, Jeannette and Samuel Reecher came to Zephyrhills and developed several citrus groves. Admiring their sumptuous grove, the Reechers strolled their property on Pretty Pond Road. Citrus groves dotted the landscape throughout the Zephyrhills area. (Courtesy of ZHA.)

The Oakside Cemetery was deeded by the Zephyrhills Colony Company to the Oakdale Cemetery Association in 1911. The name Oakdale was given to the area by John Spivey, who settled in the area after the Civil War. The cemetery markers span two centuries and mark graves from the Civil War through to the present. The entrance gate was built by Samuel J. Richards in memory of his daughter, Bernice. (Courtesy of Florida Library and Archives, Florida Department of State.)

Two

PERSONALITIES

Simon Temple came to the Starke, Florida, area in 1859 and first settled at Trail Ridge. He accumulated vast holdings of timber land, buying much of it from the government for 25¢ per acre. He moved his mill to Thurston and then Starke. The Starke area where his mill was located was commonly known as Temple Mills. He and his wife, Sarah Jane Cooley, were later persuaded to purchase land in Abbott in 1886. He seemed to have little interest in Zephyrhills once the station and section houses were built. He sold 23 lots and then mortgaged the remainder to Lydia Marvin. He returned to the Starke area. (Courtesy of Pioneer Museum.)

Dr. Joseph M. Abbott was a doctor born in Kentucky who also operated an apothecary at what is now Highway 301 and Fifth Avenue. Abbott had been a doctor in the Confederacy who was committed to saving lives and worked himself to total exhaustion. As he was near death in Texas, Abbott's friend convinced him that moving to Florida would help his convalescence. When he arrived in Zephyrhills weighing 98 pounds (quite a sight for a fellow of 6 feet, 2 inches in height), his health improved quickly, and he went into a partnership to set up a sawmill where the old Zephyr Shopping Center and the previous overpass on Highway 301 were located. Later he returned to medicine and was the proprietor of the apothecary. (Courtesy of Pioneer Museum.)

Wash day
(circa 1900)

Martha Naber labors diligently on wash day at her Zephyrhills home. This was an era of industry, jazz, silent movies (Charlie Chaplin), vaudeville, and unfortunately, the dreaded influenza, which closed schools in Zephyrhills. Change was coming to a traditional way of life for women. (Courtesy of ZHA.)

Early settlers from the Zephyrhills Colony Company camped in tents. Samuel Nyce wrote in the *Zephyrhills Colonist* on November 23, 1911, about his arrival to Zephyrhills: "The only streets opened were Fifth Avenue, and this only partially, and a few cross streets, perhaps a block. Willis Geiger had erected a house on Sixth Street above Fifth Avenue, which was then among the oaks, and several were in the course of construction. There were some tents, part tents answering for a habitation but no real homes had been erected, save those mentioned, and the greatest complaint existed. After a few days we secured lots and land and made preparations to build." (Courtesy of ZHA.)

The Zephyrhills High School girls' basketball team in 1912 was adorned in pleated black bloomers, except for a tall girl in a black dress. They were photographed by B. E. Treanor on a 1912 tour of Florida and included, from left to right, Uarda Briggs, Dorothy Briggs, Nettie Williams, Emma Williams, Mary Lisle, Azaline Geiger, Hazel Hart, Belle Adkins, Flora Shanks, Viva Brinson, and Margery Turner. (Courtesy of Delia "Dedi" Anderson.)

Capt. Howard Jeffries and his wife, Helen Mar, relax on the porch of their home. He was born in Lafayette, Indiana, and after serving in the Civil War became a reporter with the *National Tribune*. He partnered with his son-in-law, Raymond Moore, and purchased 35,000 acres at Abbott Station. On May 31, 1910, the Abbott Post Office was discontinued and the Zephyrhills Post Office instituted, beginning the official town of Zephyrhills. (Courtesy of ZHA.)

The first basketball team, in 1919, was coached by Zephyrhills principal Walter Roberts, and team members were, from left to right, (first row) Willie Stebbins, Robert Helms, and Gerald Briggs; (second row) Curtis Geiger, Warren Haynes, Fred Stebbins, Kenneth Storms, and Edwin Stebbins. This began a legacy of basketball and sports in the area. (Courtesy of Pioneer Museum.)

The Zephyrhills baseball team around 1911 included, from left to right, (first row) Roscoe Babb, Kenneth Storms (batboy), and Jimmy Boggs; (second row) George Siggins, Al Nabor, and Earl Hart; (third row) Floyd Gibson, Brant Smith, Bill Geiger, A. D. Penry (manager), Charlie Boggs, and Floyd Hennington. (Courtesy of ZHA.)

The Peni-Saver float in the 1953 Founder's Day Parade showed the enthusiasm of the town in celebrating its origins. A. D. Penry was dedicated to street beautification. This display in an annual Founder's Day Parade included driver George Green and horse Peggy as well as a rare oxen schooner. Forrest E. Hart, who had previously worked in the colony's first general store, Hennington's, opened Peni-Saver Food Store around 1937. This was the town's first self-service grocery store. (Courtesy of ZHA.)

A picnic in 1914 was a gathering for some of Zephyrhills's founders, which included, from left to right, Don Geiger, Charlie Smith, Brant Smith, Will Ryals, Floyd Hennington, unidentified, B. A. Thomas (standing), unidentified, Tom Gill, Doc Geiger, Abe Chancey, Jim Geiger, and Vernon Geiger. The original downtown park was said to be "one of the most beautiful places in the colony." The park was established in August 1911 and was originally 60 feet wide and 300 feet long. (Courtesy of Rick Moore.)

Zephyr Park was an exciting location in early Zephyrhills. Historian Genevive L. Smith wrote a poem, "If Trees Could Talk," that included, "If trees could talk . . . what would they say? / Of things so long gone by / Would they tell of glorious sunset glow / Or stormy nights when the wind would blow / Of little children neath their spreading shade / Of silent footsteps in the night / Or brilliant plumage off in flight / Think of all those stories trees could tell / 'bout sand and stars and shady dells / Your heart just wants to skip a beat / Of secret stories trees might repeat / Of peace and war, good health and pain / As protector from the sun and rain / If those trees could talk what tales they'd tell / We'd hush and listen and sit and spell / Enthralled with all the days of old / Enthralled as each sweet tale unfolds / If trees could only talk." (Courtesy of ZHA.)

After playing winter sports on an outdoor court for five decades, the first gymnasium for the community was built in 1967. In the teacher strike of 1968, nineteen area teachers took part in the Florida Education Association (FEA)–induced walkout. The state legislature and Gov. Claude Roy Kirk, supported by the superintendent, Chester Taylor, took a hard-line approach to their action, declaring it "totally unacceptable." A by-product was the closing of school for a few days and a plea to the community for certified volunteers to teach. Taylor said, "If you have a college degree or some college training . . . you are needed and will be paid $26 per day for your services." (Courtesy of ZHA.)

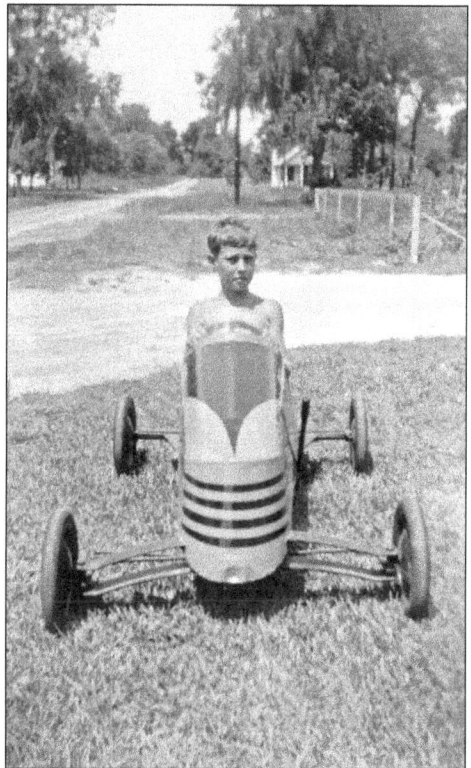

With images of racing in his head (even then), the photograph depicted race car driver Emil "Buzzie" Reutimann Jr. in his soapbox derby car as a child. The Reutimann racing family has been a legend in the Zephyrhills area. Buzzie's son, David Reutimann, currently races the family's legendary racing number 00 in NASCAR. (Courtesy of Norman Blackburn.)

With limited equipment, players had to share helmets near the end of the leatherhead helmet era, the 1947 team practices football in an open field adjacent to the school site. In this photograph are, from left to right, Richard Rosenvold, Fred LeHeup, Fred Lee Gore (in back), and James Burley. The team won the very first football game for the community against Largo in the fall of 1947. (Courtesy of the Depot Museum.)

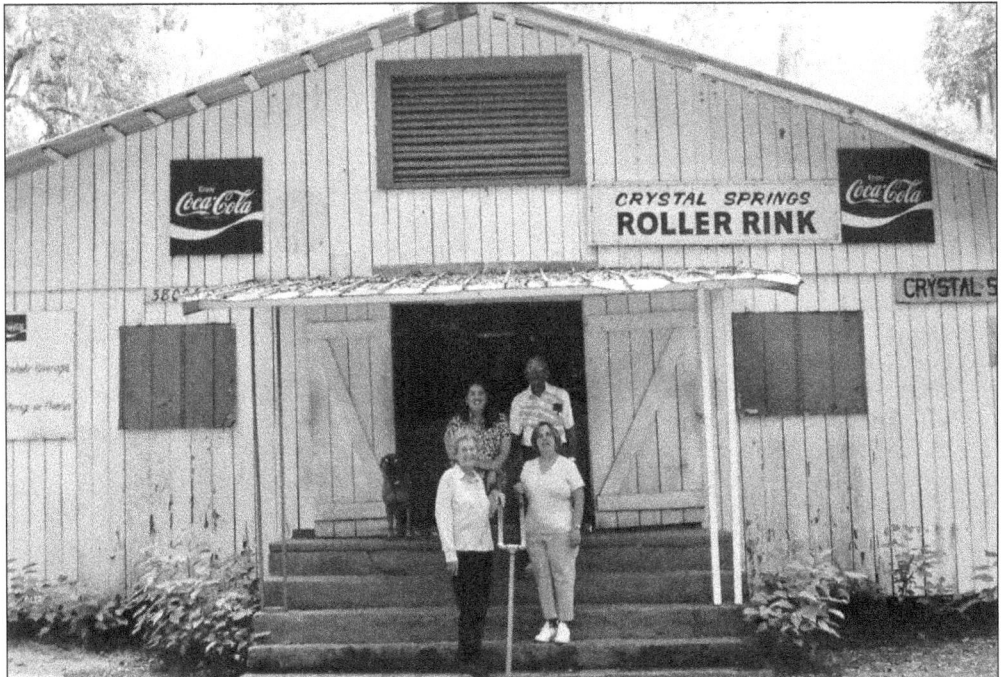

The Crystal Springs Roller Rink debuted in September 1939 and was built and opened by Walter T. Curtis, who was born in Texas. His daughter, Bernice Curtis Rooks, was almost five years old when she moved to Zephyrhills with her parents and brother. Curtis personally milled all of the rough-cut pine, which provided the signature look of the vintage Depression-era building. Opening just before World War II, the skating rink continues as a Tampa Bay–area attraction that chronicles many wonderful tales. For 35¢ in 1939, one could skate for two hours, and today for $4, a person can experience the era and get some exercise. From left to right are (first row) Bernice Curtis Rooks and Barbara Rooks Pittman; (second row) a dog, Joellyn Rooks Chancey, and Truman Rooks. (Courtesy of Clereen Morrill Brunty.)

Zephyrhills Elementary was located at the Krusen Quarters from 1949 to 1955. Students and teacher included, from left to right, (first row) Bessie Barefield (teacher/principal), Mary Etta Holmes, Wila Blue, Nancy Jones, and Mary Alice Stewart; (second row) Lonnie Turner, Bessie Mae Giles, and Mattie Holmes. (Courtesy of Irene Dobson.)

Zephyrhills suffered several fires that devastated its school buildings. When the first two-story Zephyrhills School building, between Seventh and Eighth Streets, burned to the ground in 1926, a bond issue was passed and a new $50,000 building was opened at Tenth Avenue and Tenth Street. The local newspaper reported on August 27, 1926, "It is a very pleasing structure—practically fireproof." This new stucco building, however, was severely damaged by fire in 1935, and the city banded together for two years to hold classes at local businesses that offered to host individual grades. From 1935 to 1936, high school students attended classes in a local bakery, while seventh and eighth grades were in session at the New England Hotel; the sixth grade went to class in the grocery store, third through fifth grades populated city hall, and first and second grades were schooled in the schoolhouse annex. The third Zephyrhills School building was reconstructed with the help of Roosevelt's WPA project and opened once again in 1936. (Courtesy of Rick Moore.)

The Gall brothers—from left to right, Owen, Vernon, Robert, and Louis—are proudly lined up for a photograph in posterity at Lake Zephyr on a common summer outing. Alice Hall wrote, "Walter Gall arrived in Jacksonville with his wife and children from Michigan on Thanksgiving Day, 1922 after making the trip in a Model T Ford. It is related that what with struggling through deep sand and fording unabridged streams the trip from Jacksonville to Lakeland, consumed two days. On this two-day jaunt the dream to build highways in the state of his adoption, which was later to reach fulfillment, was born." (Courtesy of ZHA.)

A mother and son are out for a leisurely walk in the first years of Zephyrhills on the first wooden bridge. This photograph predates automobiles and shows the first bridge constructed in the area—quite an engineering feat for the time period. (Courtesy of Rick Moore.)

The Zephyrhills cannon, an American field piece, was brought to Zephyrhills by Zephyr Post 118 to honor World War I veterans. They hauled it by truck from Rock Island, Illinois, and mounted it on a parkway on Main Street. It weighed 4,800 pounds. It was stationed in front of the downtown hotel for many years. During World War II, it was shipped to the scrap heap in Tampa to provide financial support for the war efforts. (Courtesy of ZHA.)

A family was out for a stroll in early Zephyrhills. Notice the businesses in the background: C. M. Totten Pool Room, South Florida Land and Timber Company, W. P. Smith's Place, and Penry's Department Store. The City Park is shown in the center and featured a full fence surrounding its area. An irrigation system and hanging lightbulbs were later features. (Courtesy of Rick Moore.)

Businessman and civic leader I. A. Krusen (front passenger's seat) leads the Founder's Day Parade in 1940. The festival began officially as "Pioneer Day" with Alice Hall and Willa Rice as cochairs of sponsoring groups—Lion's Club, Garden Club, and Women's Club. Willa dressed as well-known Simon Legree (also known as "old Snag"), with a committee reenacted a holdup of Skinner's Drug Store and then Neukom's, followed by a mock train robbery of the Seaboard Coast Line. (Courtesy of Florida Library and Archives, Florida Department of State.)

Vacation Bible school illustrated the cohesiveness of the day and traditional values of the community. A long history of religious focus in the community spawned vacation Bible school, which began in the First Baptist Church of Zephyrhills around 1898. Programs included crafts, recreation, refreshments, and Bible games. The Bible schools were somewhat influenced by the Bible Belt. (Courtesy of Clereen Morrill Brunty.)

Rosemary Wallace Trottman was the 1985 grand marshal of the Zephyrhills Founder's Day Parade. Trottman published *The History of Zephyrhills 1821–1921* in 1978 and served as a teacher in Zephyrhills schools for many years. Trottman founded the Zephyrhills Historical Association, whose inaugural meeting was July 23, 1980. (Courtesy of ZHA.)

Mayor Willa Rice has the distinction of being the only female mayor of Zephyrhills, and she served from 1957 to 1960. In the photograph, Mayor Rice (standing) addresses, from left to right, city councilmen Paul Shultz, Sam Surratt, Bernard E. Burns, James Jarrett, and Albert C. Hooks. (Courtesy of ZHA.)

Alice Fryer Hall was an icon in the Zephyrhills community. She relocated to Zephyrhills from her native Mississippi in 1941 and lived on a farm on Fort King Road with her husband, Melville. As an activist in civic and political clubs, she was also a columnist for the *Zephyrhills News* and *Tampa Tribune*. She organized the Zephyrhills Community Blood Bank. This photograph captures Alice in a playful moment in which she was dressed in 19th-century garb and playfully reenacted a pioneer woman's experiences. (Courtesy of ZHA.)

The most prestigious of the annual parades has traditionally been the one commemorating the city's founding. In 1970, Miss Zephyrhills, Lois Ann Wells, led the parade. The Miss Zephyrhills Pageant dates back to 1927. Wells, a skilled dancer, became a local celebrity as she went on to "kick up her heels" as a star in the New York City Rockettes. (Courtesy of ZHA.)

The *Spotlight* annual staff of the Zephyrhills School produced a mimeographed book in 1935. The staff included editor Vera Cook and, from left to right, (first row) Donald Plank, Red "Leslie" Chilson, Rebecca Magness, Marguerite Snyder, Norma Stone, Harmon "H. D." Pollock, and Emil Reutimann; (second row) Eva West, two unidentified, Ruth McCoy, unidentified, Margaret Slater, unidentified, and Margie Reutimann: (third row) Andy Sullivan and Fred Wheeler. Other members were Vernon Childers, Mary Emery, Ernest Linkey, Sarah A. Clardy, Laura Rogers, Irene Lefler, Evelyn Mundy, Helen Lefler, Gilbert Chenkins, L. B. Nettles, Richard Gaskin, Minnie Slater, and teacher/advisor Lilla A. Taylor. (Courtesy of ZHA.)

The Municipal Swimming Pool was built through the WPA and opened June 1, 1939. Admission to the pool was 5¢, and for an additional 10¢, one could sign up for swimming lessons. (Courtesy of Mary Lou Massey.)

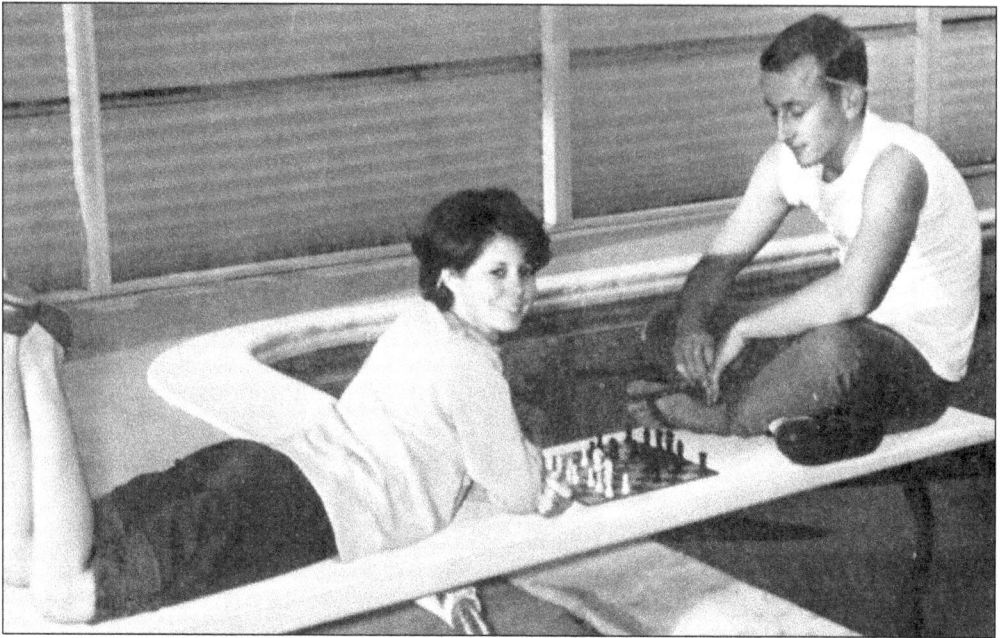

A swim in 1964 was the highlight of a summer day. At its opening on June 1, 1939, admission to the pool was 5¢. The configuration of the pool was quite efficient—a baby pool was available for young children, sloping from 8 inches to 17 inches; the main pool had a gradual incline to 10 feet deep with two diving boards. The VFW Hall served as the dressing room area. Mary Lou "Cookie" Massey was their most notable lifeguard; she went on to become a mermaid at Weeki Wachee Springs. Others mentioned were Casey Kearse, J. W. Wells, Clayton Stokes, and Glenn Miller, and local coaches were Bill Kustes, Ann Crawford, and Thomas Webb. Photographed here are Jere Alston and Jim Daniels. (Courtesy of ZHS.)

School students in the 1930s pose in front of the second school building in the Zephyrhills area. School sports players were referred to as Zephyrs, not the Bulldogs. The local newspaper, the *Pasco Free Press*, featured a weekly school news insert, the *Orange and Black*, which lobbied for various programs including a football team (which was not to come to fruition until 1941) and also wrote editorials in support of the establishment of a home economics curriculum and vocational training. (Courtesy of Clereen Morrill Brunty.)

50

Home economics students hosted the school trustees of Zephyrhills in 1946 for the annual banquet, which demonstrated their culinary skills and hostessing expertise. Girls had classes in a separate cottage location for their cooking, sewing, and home management courses. (Courtesy of ZHS.)

John F. Clements Field, the home football field on County Road 54 East, was dedicated to Coach Clements. In 1988, Clements's record was recognized by the FHSAA for being only one of five high school coaches in the United States with a winning record of more than 400 games. A man of strong family values, Clements and his wife, Marvene ("Beanie"), celebrated their 66th wedding anniversary in 2009. They have two children, John II and Diane, and two grandchildren, Johnny III and Kim McGavern. (Courtesy of ZHS.)

Mary Lou Richards was the only mermaid from Zephyrhills. A promotional pamphlet of 1954–1955 proclaimed, "Weeki Wachee proudly presents an Underwater Fantasy," and explained that the show took place at 70 feet below the surface, putting mermaids in a pressurized water situation of danger while performing their underwater ballet. (Courtesy of Mary Lou Massey.)

Shuffleboard courts dotted the Zephyrhills landscape and had their origins with the Tourist Club. Notice the formal dress for the game in the 1930s. (Courtesy of Rick Moore.)

The Red Cross, a group of young people in 1968, was a service organization popular for many years. "School Daze" columnist Dedi Anderson reported in October 1959, "Unusually active this year is the Junior Red Cross, under President Judy Surratt, who attended a National Red Cross Leadership Camp this summer. Officers Lorene Daughtery and Susan Gill helped in giving a coffee for all teachers. At a surprise assembly, Judy Goulding, Lynn Nichols, J. W. Wells and Norman Weaver took part in a pantomime which urged the students 'not to let Red Cross die.' " (Courtesy of ZHS.)

One could travel on the Seaboard Air Line, with its corporate motto, "The Route of Courteous Service." In the first half of the 20th century, Seaboard, along with its main competitor, Atlantic Coast Line Railroad, contributed greatly to the economic development of Florida. Its primary revenues derived from bringing vacationers to Florida from the Northeast and carrying Southern timber, minerals, and produce, especially Florida citrus crops, to the Northern states. (Courtesy of Rick Moore.)

Produce was loaded regularly onto the Seaboard Coast Line train. Workers loaded watermelons grown near Zephyrhills. The sign on the building reads "Pasco Fruit Company." The lettering on the truck says "M. M. Lee Grower Citrus Fruits and Watermelons." There is a sticker on the back of the picture that says "#4 grower's truck Port Richie FL." (Courtesy of Florida Library and Archives, Florida Department of State.)

Christine Douglas shows off her catch during a fishing expedition. Douglas said that her father, I. A. Krusen, bought 13,000 acres, mostly on credit, for $2.75 per acre. This was the beginning of Krusen Land and Timber Company. He built a sawmill and paid off the land by selling lumber. Christine said her father, known by his friends as Andy, first bought 40 acres where he built the sawmill, their family home, and a number of tenant dwellings. Krusen also built a company store. "I used to work there on Saturday mornings, sacking up sugar, beans and grits," Christine recalled. "They really loved them and asked where they could buy some. My dad loved to tease people and he gave them a bag of grits. He said when you go home, plant them and you can grow grits." (Courtesy of Florida Library and Archives, Florida Department of State.)

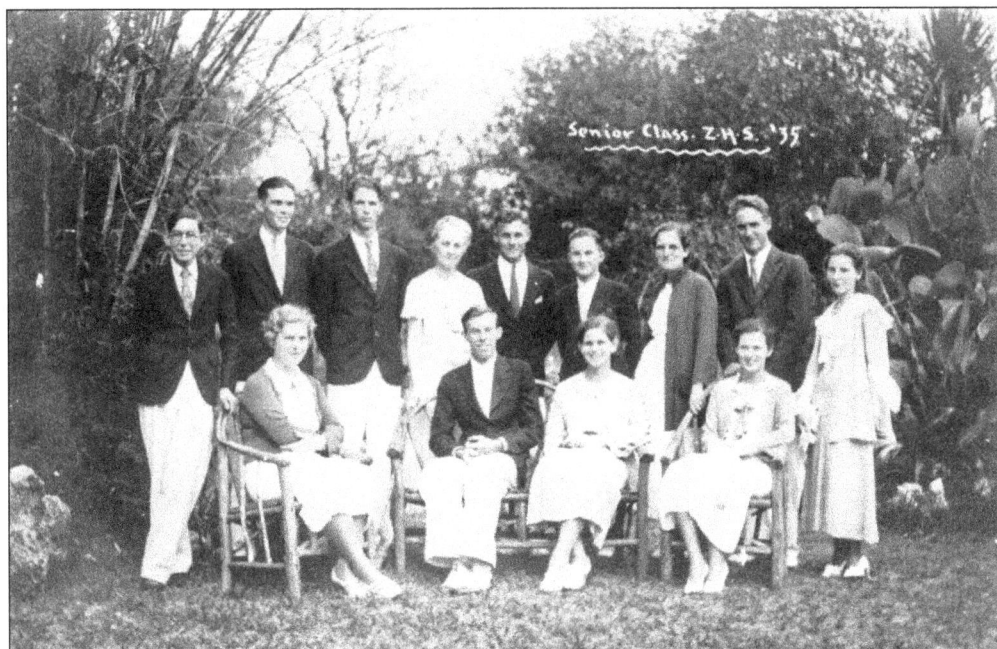

An official portrait announced the local graduating class of 1935, posed as if they were starring in *The Great Gatsby*. The class roster included Sara Parsons, Rebecca Magness, Eva West, Mary Emery, Frances Vogel, Ernest Linkey, Emil Reutimann Jr., Harmon Pollock, Leslie Chilson, Richard Gaskins, Fred Wheeler, Donald Plank, Ruth McCoy, Laura Rogers, Emma Rose Wingate, and Jack Parsons. (Courtesy of Delia "Dedi" Anderson.)

The Peepleses were proprietors of a department store in Zephyrhills for many years and were very involved in the community's development. The party of local residents in the photograph includes, from left to right, (seated) Hap and Jeannette Cherry; (standing) Merrill Cherry, Corrine Sumner Peeples, Logan Peeples, and Margaret Nelson Cherry. (Courtesy of Margaret Nelson Cherry.)

Tillie Reutimann Smith looked out her window over the fairways of Silver Oaks, which used to be the "Little Pasture;" it was a long way and a long time from the "Big Pasture" where she would do the family laundry by building a fire under the backyard iron wash kettle. Brantley, the patriarch of the Smith family, was one of the original members of the Florida Citrus Commission. (Courtesy of ZHA.)

The *News* wrote, "Miss Anna Jo Davis, wearing an elegant purple and gold robe over her pretty red formal to reign over the pageant, placed the crown from her head on that of her successor and transferred the royal robe to Linda Sabo's shoulders to climax the event." Miss Davis was Miss Zephyrhills of 1963. The robe was made for the Lion's Club by Mrs. Lee G. Cass. Anna Jo Davis Bracknell is wife of former city councilman Clyde Bracknell and was an educator in the town for many years. (Courtesy of ZHS.)

Judge Richard Kelly gained state and national fame as a marine, circuit judge, west central Florida congressman, and ultimately as a victim of the FBI Abscam sting; his affiliation to ZHS was something that Kelly prided himself on until his death in 2005. He was a member of the very first school football team in 1941, coached by the school principal, Thomas Burch Cornelius. Kelly was the keynote speaker at the ground-breaking of the current ZHS campus in 1975. (Courtesy of Florida Library and Archives, Florida Department of State.)

The Zephyrhills Army Airfield was constructed as part of a group of state and WPA projects. Major expansion of the airfield began in 1941, when it became home to U.S. Army Air Corps training facilities in preparation for World War II. It was in full operation in 1943, providing advanced fighter pilot training to air crews destined for service in Europe. A common 1940s sight was servicemen in town. The GI is Charlie Sante. (Courtesy of Linda Sante.)

Dr. Catherine Cornelius is the daughter of school principal Thomas Burch Cornelius, who served on the Draft Board (after volunteering to enter the World War II military service and being refused because the military board said Cornelius would be more valuable to the war effort by continuing to serve as principal). She said that her mother remembered pilots being trained near Zephyrhills and the sky literally full of airplanes nearly all the time. Many soldiers were on the streets of Zephyrhills and nearby when they had time off from their training. (Courtesy of Linda Sante.)

A bus driver poses with the first local school bus that was not pulled by horse or oxen serving the Zephyrhills Schools. (Courtesy of Elizabeth Geiger.)

The Racing Reutimann, pictured in the 1950s with their racing fleet, included, from left to right, Emil Reutimann and sons Dale, Wayne, and Buzzie, who stand by their cars. Actual stock car racing in the Reutimann family goes back to 1938, when Emil Jr. raced a hot rod at the Ben White Speedway in Orlando. (Courtesy of ZHS.)

A photograph from Wayman's Studio in Zephyrhills shows various groups of Zephyrhills residents. Bob Jensen and F. L. Garrison wrote in their piece "From Pioneers Sowed County's Growth," "A big change in Pasco came after World War II, when retirees began to come from colder lands in the north. 'Quality of life'—translated as affordable housing and warm weather—changed the face of Pasco. The '$5,990' helped spur the post-war boom. That was the typical cost of Pasco's standard two-bedroom house, a price that made retirement affordable. Northern tourists who were enamored after vacationing on the more pricey beaches to the south found themselves wondering how they could afford to make their home in the Florida sun." (Courtesy of Rick Moore.)

Peter E. Bobb and his wife, Peula, were early Zephyrhills settlers. They operated Summy's House and also farmed just outside of the town. In addition, they operated a lumberyard. The photograph on the front cover also shows Bobb's Wisconsin Rooming House when it was earlier known as Summy's. (Courtesy of ZHA.)

Don Robinson was the founder of Zephyrhills Bottled Water. In 1961, Don Robinson took advantage of Zephyrhills's important natural resource: good-tasting water. He founded the Zephyrhills Corporation, which through its bottled water spread the name of Zephyrhills all over Florida. In 1987, Nestlé Waters North America bought him out, and the company has taken the brand worldwide. (Courtesy of ZHS.)

Celia Linkey Anderson, a 1929 ZHS graduate, was a Florida State University graduate and also library director and Latin teacher at Zephyrhills High. During the last 10 years of her career, she held the position of library science professor at the University of South Florida. She wrote *The History of Education in Pasco County.* (Courtesy of Delia "Dedi" Anderson.)

At the 2005 demolition of the school building (built in 1926), many alumni attended a final open house and sealed away some vital memories of their schooling and childhood experiences. The group posed in front of the school for one final memory and narrated anecdotes about their school experiences that ran the gamut from inspirational teachers to paddlings. (Courtesy of Clereen Morrill Brunty.)

Brownie Troop 267 marched in the 1962 Founder's Day Parade with Girl Scout Troop 429 at the rear. Their troop leader, Bobbie Lou Hormuth, a veteran educator, gazes over at Sheila Hormuth. From left to right, the Scouts are (first row) Sheila Hormuth, Jenell Stell Welsch (holding banner), and Bobbie Lou Hormuth; (second row) Judi Dunnigan, Cherie Wilson, Martha Miller, and unidentified; (third row) Clereen Morrill at far left; (fourth row) Phyllis Jarrett at far left; (fifth row) helper Elaine Howard; (sixth row) Assistant Scout Troop Leader Vera Morrill. (Courtesy of Clereen Morrill Brunty.)

The high school girls' basketball team was coached by Celia Linkey Anderson (at right). Celia's daughter, Dedi Anderson, reported that the principal, James Theodore Campbell Jr. (gentleman with white shirt), recruited Anderson to coach the basketball team. She had never played basketball and so proceeded to learn it from an instructional book. In regard to the manner in which tradition and learning was passed from generation to generation, Dedi shared with the author that one of the members of Anderson's girls' basketball team was Willette Phillips of the Willie Taxi Company, who went on to be a donor to sports in the city. (Courtesy of Delia "Dedi" Anderson.)

May 1938

The first airmail deliveries came to Zephyrhills in 1938. It cost $5 for postage, and Mayor B. F. Parsons and Dr. B. A. Thomas received the airmail letter, mailed by postmaster Lola D. Gall from Lakeland. The location was adjoining Lake Zephyr by the Winters' Park, and the pilot was a Mr. Pollock. In 1946, the local high school senior class even purchased a BT-13 Vultee Trainer airplane from the war surplus supply to provide an aeronautics curriculum at the school. In the 21st century, Zephyrhills is known for its world-class parachute center at Zephyrhills Airport. (Courtesy of ZHA.)

Judge James Wilton Sanders's daughter, Johnnye Mae Sanders Entz (right), spoke at an interview at her home in Dade City and displayed the declarations and honors given to her father. Conducting the interviews were Clereen Morrill Brunty (left) and Wise (center). Entz recalled that Sanders was a large man in stature—6 foot, 2 inches—with a stern demeanor and the heart of an outdoorsman. He loved to hunt and fish. Later elected school superintendent and county judge, Sanders worked tirelessly on the consolidation of schools in Pasco County as well. (Courtesy of Clereen Morrill Brunty.)

The first principal of the consolidated Zephyrhills Schools was Judge Sanders. A plaque in recognition of Sanders is posted at the Lacoochee School House Exhibit at the Dade City Pioneer Museum. The plaque contains a memoriam and a biography of Sanders that highlights his role as the first principal. Officials (between 1913 and 1921) were, from left to right, (seated) L. J. Gaskin, school board member; and J. W. Sanders, county superintendent of schools; (standing) Sid Larkin and W. E. Douglas, school board member. (Courtesy of Pioneer Museum.)

A very early high school group proudly poses. From left to right are (first row) Belle Adkins, Hazel Hart, Flora Shanks, Uarda Briggs, Mary Lisle, Blanche Geiger, Viva Brinson, and Margery Turner; (second row) George Orcutt, Leo Ecker, Jeffrey Turner (above Uarda), unidentified, Lula Ryals, unidentified, Billy Siggins, and Simon Geiger. (Courtesy of Pioneer Museum.)

Three

THE UNIQUE CULTURE
OF ZEPHYRHILLS

The signature Zephyrhills camphor tree was planted 119 years ago by Capt. James Polk Renfroe, a Florida pioneer, who engineered the first railroad locomotive from Fernandina Beach to Tampa. Captain Renfroe brought his wife and three sons in 1881 from Blakshear, Georgia. He ordered some trees and shrubs from Washington, D.C., and in the shipment was a small camphor tree (about 12 inches), which Agnes Renfroe planted on March 3, 1890, the day before her daughter, Agnes Roberts, was born. Captain Renfroe was a hearty pioneer in Zephyrhills and one of the first to develop land. (Courtesy of Ernest Wise.)

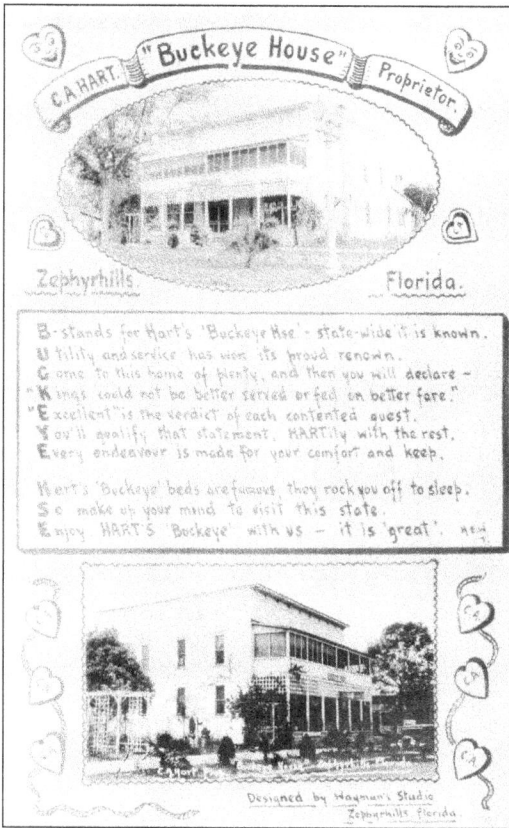

B-stands for Hart's 'Buckeye Hse' - state-wide it is known.
Utility and service has won its proud renown.
Come to this home of plenty, and then you will declare –
"Kings could not be better served or fed on better fare."
"Excellent" is the verdict of each contented guest.
You'll qualify that statement, HARTily with the rest.
Every endeavour is made for your comfort and keep.

Hart's 'Buckeye' beds are famous, they rock you off to sleep.
So make up your mind to visit this state.
Enjoy HART'S 'Buckeye' with us – it is 'great'. NEW

Designed by Wayman's Studio
Zephyrhills Florida

A popular location throughout the town's early history was the Zephyr Hotel. Its first name was the Buckeye House, and the proprietor was C. A. Hart. An innovative advertisement was prepared by Wayman's Studio of Zephyrhills and includes an acronym: "B-uckeye House, statewide it is known; U-tility and service . . . ; C-ome to this home of plenty and then you will declare K-ings could not do better . . . ; E-xcellent is the verdict . . . ; Y-ou'll qualify that statement, heartily . . . ; E-very endeavor is made for your comfort." (Courtesy of Rick Moore.)

Down-to-earth land values, a favorable tax structure, and flat ground with room for expansion attracted dairymen to the area. The Palm River Dairy, originally founded by Ignazio Spoto in 1902, was a family dairy; Joe Spoto and his wife, Frances, are depicted in the photograph. Other dairies included B. Lee Gore, H. W. Dean, Walter Rowland, and Neil Rucks. Bennett Lee Gore and his wife, Mary Vick, with their two sons, Fred and John, moved to Zephyrhills in 1943 to first lease a dairy and in 1944 purchase an operation. That location on Highway 301 recently became the Zephyr Commons Shopping Area. (Courtesy of Maria Spoto.)

The Zephyrhills Theater was a popular location. Depicted on Main Street in the 1940s, there was a bit of irony in the popular film listed on the marquee, *It Happened Tomorrow*. It continues to operate today. (Courtesy of Phyllis Geiger Debien.)

The names on the truck banner in front of Memorial Hall in 1938 were City Drug Store (C. C. Daniels); Walter Gall Real Estate; Zephyrhills Post Office (Lola Gall); George Storm's Seeds/ Feeds; Penry's Dry Goods; Judge O. L. Dayton Jr., Hamilton Feed Store; Reichart Barber; Pasco Sheriff's Office (Sheriff Otis Allen); Krusen Land and Timber Company; Jack Booth Crate Mill; Wayman's Studio; Thomas No. 1 Shoe Repair; Francis Sibley Plumbing; Standard Service Station (Art Vogel); Sunrise Place (J. Moore); Gill's Texaco Station; Darby's Grocery; Geiger Mercantile Company; Zephyr Theater (C. E. Bailey); and Ann's Lunch Place. The truck was inscribed with "W. T. Curtis Lumber and Manufacturing Company." (Courtesy of ZHA.)

This lively march down the main part of town memorialized Armistice Day Parade in Zephyrhills in the early 1940s. In the background, one can see Hotel Zephyr, which served as a central location for entertainment and guests. (Courtesy of Phyllis Geiger Debien.)

The city park compound was developed in 1920 and temporarily closed during the Great Depression. Zephyrhills in 1920s was growing. School principal Ptolemy W. Corr advertised in the local newspaper, the *Colonist*, for families to board local students. In March 1921, he wrote, "I beg of you to throw your homes open to the Normal students for the common normal. The hotels and boarding houses have done this, but a great many students prefer to board in private homes. Respectfully, P. W. Corr." (Courtesy of Rick Moore.)

Looking like a "wild west town," the downtown in 1911 housed emporiums of commerce. Founders of the colony expected that Seventh Street between Fifth and Fourth Avenues would remain "Main Street," but the block today contains mainly the Tourist Club. Notice that the picture includes a barber pole and water pump to the right. (Courtesy of ZHA.)

Cane grinding and boiling was necessary. This picture portrays syrup making with the boiling vat and a mule in the background. Isaac Cripe reported that they "had a sugar cane grinding rig in their pasture and growers would haul their cane to be ground and cooked into syrup. The enterprise was usually done on shares. Sugar cane syrup was almost like money, selling for $1 a gallon. Fifty gallons of syrup could be traded for a pony." (Courtesy of Florida Library and Archives, Florida Department of State.)

Opened on March 12, 1912, the original bank was the First State Bank, incorporated by McCormick, Stapleton, and Company. Its motto was "A Home Institution Means Progress for You." This institution was a victim of the Great Depression and closed abruptly. Another bank did not open until 1949. (Courtesy of the Depot Museum.)

The fish pond, a special feature at the Zephyrhills School, was constructed by George McGinnis and one of his sons, James Douglas McGinnis. It was built prior to 1949. George's daughter Donah McGinnis Neal and son Herbert McGinnis described their recollection of the signature pond: "It was approximately eight feet horizontally, and made of stone. There was a dome that covered approximately one-third of the pond to provide shade." They marvel to this day at how their dad was able to build that free-standing dome. McGinnis also built several other ponds for Zephyr Park, one of which had a bridge walkway. The ponds were stocked with koi (goldfish). The sophomore officers of 1951 sit on top of the fishpond in this photograph. (Courtesy of ZHS.)

Children are shown playing at Zephyr Park. Simon Geiger reported that before World War I, Zephyrhills held big community celebrations on George Washington's birthday and on Independence Day each year. On these two days, the cattlemen of the area would donate beef for a big barbecue, and there would be horse races and a baseball game. The whole community turned out for these big occasions. (Courtesy of Rick Moore.)

This photograph, titled "A Refreshing Drink in Zephyr Lake," shows that the water was great for the animals as well as human residents. (Courtesy of Rick Moore.)

Imagine the early parades that passed by Hotel Row with the various local dignitaries of the day. The first documented Miss Zephyrhills was Lucile Ryals in 1927. She was selected through a community vote. The *News* (formerly the *Colonist*) of September 29, 1927, was filled with information about the contest, coronation, and parade. The total number of votes polled for all candidates in the 1927 contest was 996,450 (obviously, they did multiple voting). (Courtesy of Rick Moore.)

Later Hotel Row Zephyrhills had a remarkable Quarterback Club composed of businessmen and civic leaders who guided sports development. The Quarterback Club was organized in 1941 to promote athletics in an athletics-less school, with Charles E. Gibson as the first president. The name was changed in 1979 to the Booster Club. This group was responsible for nearly every sports innovation that occurred throughout the town's sports history. (Courtesy of ZHA.)

The city hall contained the police station and two jail cells. The location was mentioned in much of the history. The *News* reported in January 1939 "that a parade to advance the infantile paralysis campaign marched with Irene Hohenthaner as drum major down Fifth Avenue and to city hall, where it disbanded. The students were glad to learn that their behavior was good and as a result school was dismissed forty-five minutes earlier on Monday afternoon." (Courtesy of Rick Moore.)

A view of Fifth Avenue causes one to reflect. The city had no government from 1910 until 1914. The local Welfare League and Board of Trade met weekly. (Courtesy of ZHA.)

The Women's Club (earlier known as the Welfare League and the Women's Civic League) was established in 1915. The building was a component of the WPA project and was crafted from limestone. The club first met at the present location on April 18, 1941. It continues to host weddings, meetings, and community events. (Courtesy of Ernest Wise.)

Stone Cabins Court was south of town on the west side of Highway 301. A novelty, it featured individual buildings with private rooms and baths built of native limestone rock. (Courtesy of ZHA.)

Standing at city hall, one could catch a sweep of the town in the 1950s. Occupants over time in the city hall building included Massey's Barbershop, PhotoCraft, and Sue's Sew Shop. (Courtesy of Rick Moore.)

The *News* reported on February 4, 1938, that the Zephyr Post 118 was in place: "The veterans 'from over there' had an enthusiastic meeting last Saturday and selected officers who included: George MacMillan, Commander; J. W. Booth, Roy Hart, George Ross, Don Storms, Jack Schernau, and Stanley Hammond." (Courtesy of ZHA.)

First Baptist Church predates the development of Zephyrhills. The Six Mile Pond Baptist Church met at Abbott on January 5, 1902, for the purpose of organizing a church to be inaugurated as Lakeview Baptist Church of Abbott. Lakeview Baptist Church then became First Baptist Church, and the current site was chosen. The original portion of the present church was constructed in 1928 and cost $30,000. The News reported, "The building is one of the most pretentious in the whole county. It has a foundation of cement and the exterior is of light buff brick." (Courtesy of ZHA.)

The First Methodist Church began in 1912 with Rev. N. J. Hawley and met in homes until this building was constructed in 1913. Here it is surrounded by automobiles. (Courtesy of ZHA.)

76

Tourist Club - Zephyrhills, Fla.   2-H-576

The Tourist Club of Zephyrhills had the motto "To promote good fellowship among its members and to foster a community spirit favorable to the best interests of the Club and the City of Zephyrhills." The activities included ballroom dancing, square dancing, shuffleboard, horseshoes, card parties, and entertainment. (Courtesy of ZHA.)

Seventh Street, Zephyrhills, Fla.

This is Seventh Street. A promotional article about the city of Zephyrhills in the October 1930 *News* read, "What Others Say and Think of Zephyrhills—'It [Zephyrhills] restored my health,' declared New England Publisher; 'you can get more for less money in Zephyrhills than in any other place I know of,' stated Lieutenant Colonel Wheeler, USA Retired; while a large Massachusetts Newspaper said, 'The cost of living in Zephyrhills is only half that of other places. Health conditions of school children are good due to the fine water and citrus fruits.' " (Courtesy of ZHA.)

Looking down Main Street from the State Bank corner in the 1920s, one could ponder. The local 1929 basketball team went to the state tournament for the first time in history. In the final championship game against St. Petersburg, the five players had a lead at halftime but fell behind in the second half after one of the stars, Louie Evans, broke out with chicken pox during intermission. Today players are allowed five fouls, but Cecil McGavern recalled that he finished the game with seven fouls after the captain of the St. Pete team gave his permission for McGavern to stay in the game. The team was undefeated, losing only the last state tournament game. (Courtesy of ZHA.)

Mayor B. F. Parsons published an open letter to winter guests in the *News* on February 26, 1937: "Many of you have long made Zephyrhills the seat of your winter sojourns and liked it here for as the birds, you return season after season. May we ask when you go home that you will disseminate these facts to your friends that may be prospective visitors: That Zephyrhills is an unusually healthy place in which to live; That Zephyrhills has a fine and pure a water supply as can be found in the state; That we have a high school of unexcelled rating, and a degreed faculty; That most of the leading fraternal organizations have lodges here; That nine churches with good congregations and able pastors; That we have a colony of happy, contented Spanish American War Veterans in our midst, with Camp and Auxiliary units." (Courtesy of ZHA.)

Prof. Austin B. Morris was quite an accomplished horse trainer, an equestrian, and a veterinarian from New York. He and his wife, Jane, initiated the Professor Morris Museum—quite an attraction in Zephyrhills—with lots of taxidermy and compilations. It was located at the corner of Fifth Avenue and Second Street. (Courtesy of ZHA.)

A view of the park on Main Street caused James Kenyon to reflect that in his class of 1916 he was the only boy with four pretty girl classmates. Also he was the captain of the boys' basketball team, which was undefeated his senior year. (Courtesy of ZHA.)

This 1923 postcard of Zephyrhills is entitled "Band Stand, Zephyrhills, Florida." By 1923, the town was no longer referred to as a colony. Author Rosemary Trottman related that colonists had begun to speak of themselves as pioneers by this decade and referred to the 1840–1910 settlers as the natives. An annual community Christmas tree program was held each year at the bandstand park, which had just installed a well and septic tank. (Courtesy of the Depot Museum.)

Stevens Hall adjoined the Methodist church and was a meeting place for all types of groups (such as Home Demonstration Agent workshops, Boys and Girls Club, Women's Club, school receptions, and more). (Courtesy of ZHA.)

Four

INSTITUTIONS

Just south of Zephyrhills is Fort Foster, one of the locations from the Second Seminole War, also known as the Florida War (1835–1842). This replica wooden fort was constructed on the original fort location and hosts annual rendezvous, skirmishes, and seasonal events in the Florida parkland surrounded by native flora and wildlife. (Courtesy of Ernest Wise.)

A. W. OBSERVATION POST. ZEPHYRHILLS. FLA.

This World War II observation tower was indicative of structures in the 1940s that were built in part for security. This handsome structure was located at what later housed the chamber of commerce. (Courtesy of Rick Moore.)

A 1930 photograph of I. A. Krusen at the Krusen Land and Timber Company in Zephyrhills reveals the mill and millwork, a major industry. (Courtesy of Florida Library and Archives, Florida Department of State.)

Vintage cars parked at the Krusen Land and Timber Company in Zephyrhills in 1930 showed the lumber mill and millwork building. (Courtesy of Florida Library and Archives, Florida Department of State.)

The Krusen homestead in the 1930s was reflective of the era; the group in front includes, from left to right, Mary Ann Grieves Walker, Betty Tomczak, Julie Blakeske Barron, Dorothy Barron Krusen, Christine Skinner Krusen, and I. A. Krusen. (Courtesy of Florida Library and Archives, Florida Department of State.)

Zephyrhills had a water booth by the depot for many years. As the "city of pure water," this was a place to get a jug of cool fresh water. Notice the sign on the water booth that proclaimed, "Have a glass of our pure water, free!" (Courtesy of ZHA.)

Krusen Field, a public athletic field in Zephyrhills, was built in the 1940s by Mayor I. A. Krusen. It was named for his son, Charles B. Krusen, who loved sports. The field hosted the football team for many years and was the scene of the Easter sunrise services annually sponsored by the Ministerial Association. In later years, Florida Hospital Zephyrhills hosted the annual sunrise service. (Courtesy of Ernest Wise.)

Post Office and Frazier's Sweet Shop, Zephyrhills, Fla.

The post office was combined with Frazier's Sweet Shop, and the inaugural city postmaster was James Geiger, known around town as "Uncle Jim." He was also an owner of a general store and a councilman. The photograph is from 1922. (Courtesy of ZHA.)

The library building was on Sixth Street. It was first organized in 1912 by a group of citizens in a room of the GAR building. They began with 77 books. In 1915, a piece of land was purchased from First Christian Church for $75. Anna Hartman was the first paid librarian. Until 1949, library work was done by volunteers. (Courtesy of ZHA.)

Mary Shepard donated about 2.5 acres to the city for a children's playground in 1919. She specified that no games of chance or alcoholic drinks be allowed, nor play on Sunday. Shepard Park has been home to the Scouting program in the area. (Courtesy of Ernest Wise.)

Hercules Powder Company was a major employer from the time it was established in 1946 until it closed in 1962. They harvested pine stumps, which were sent to Brunswick, Georgia, to be processed for resin and pine oil. The national umbrella of the company established what was known at Hercules Powder Company Camp No. 39 on an 80-acre tract north of the city. (Courtesy of Pioneer Museum.)

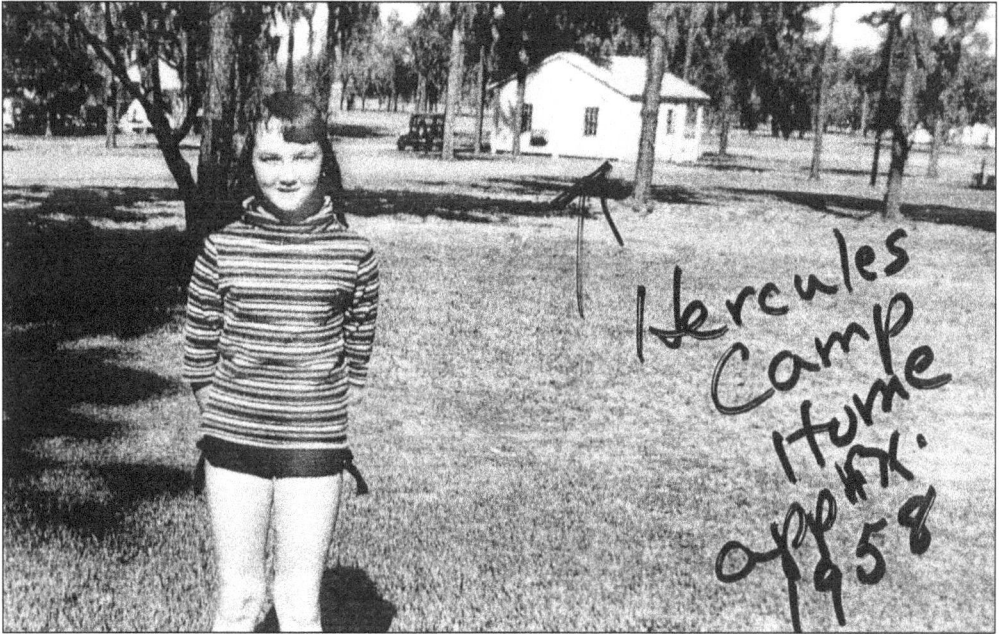

Hercules Powder Company provided housing for 42 families who lived on the grounds. The property was located on what became Woodland Elementary School, ZHS, and the Hercules Aquatic Center. Several of the actual houses were moved when the site was closed in 1962 and remain in the Zephyrhills area. The girl who posed in the photograph is Carol Grace Reffitt; her father, Thomas Grace, was employed by Hercules for many years, according to Harriett Morton Weicht, whose father worked at Hercules as well. (Courtesy of Pioneer Museum.)

Stanley Kendrick was a vocational teacher in the local school for over 30 years. One of his students, Janet Johnson Cruver, wrote in 1957, "Because of his big heart and enormous love for children and young people, students felt his concern and the fact that he truly cared about them. Speaking for the thousands he mentored, thank you Mr. Kendrick and may there be more like you!" (Courtesy of ZHS.)

Speaking of water towers, here is a bird's-eye view of the town in the late 1920s, showing the original wooden water tower. Some may not know there were two Seventh Streets, with the railroad running between them. (Courtesy of ZHA.)

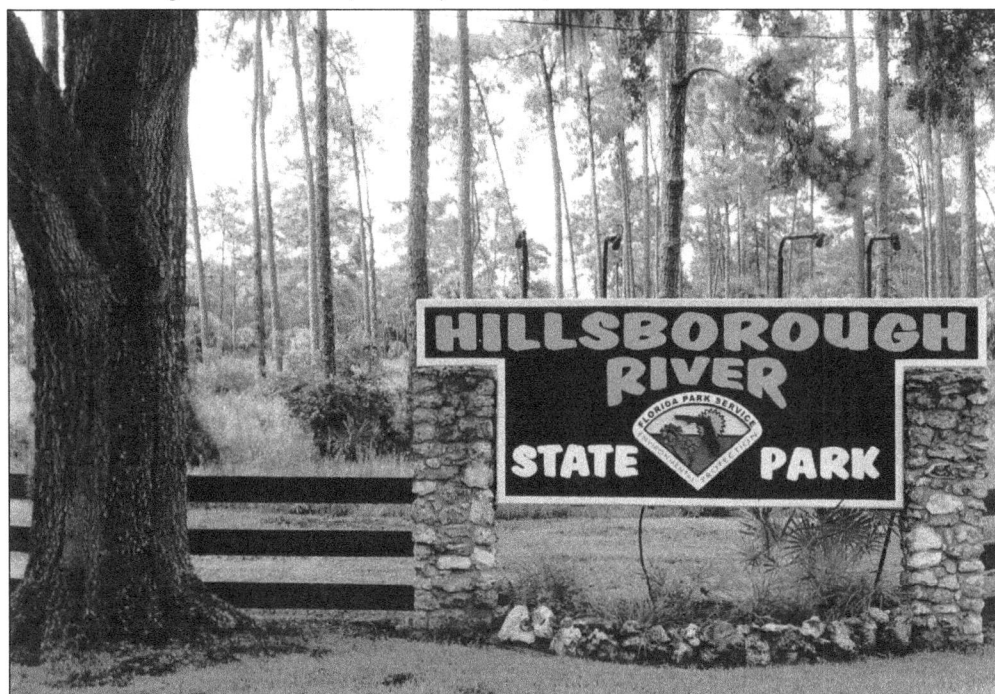

Hillsborough State Park was built in 1936 by the Civilian Conservation Corps, a component of the New Deal. It has been an attraction of the area for many years. Stories of lifeguarding at the park abound. It offered a historical feature, Fort Foster, which commemorated a military fort near the site that was instrumental in the Second Seminole War. The photograph is from the 1940s and shows the entrance marker, which remains the same in 2009. (Courtesy of Rick Moore.)

Of Elsie's Dime Store, Diane Clements Vilas said, "As a little kid, I could walk around town in complete safety. I'd walk from the municipal pool into town and if I had a few coins, I'd head to Neukom's, Elsie's 5 and 10, or Lamb's Toy Store and I would pass by Willie's Taxi. You could watch the goldfish in the rock pond or stop for a cold sip from the only water fountain in town." (Courtesy of ZHA.)

In 1935, this building was called the U.S. War Pasco Veterans Camp. It had been constructed in 1910 as the original GAR Hall, which also served as the first public auditorium and movie house. It was made of heart pine, cut from Greer's Mill and transported by oxcart. It exists today as the American Legion Hall. (Courtesy of Rick Moore.)

The second official bank in Zephyrhills, the Bank of Zephyrhills, hosted a reception at its opening on November 11, 1949. It was built by Krusen Construction Company and was the first bank in Zephyrhills since the 1928 collapse of the first financial institution. For the opening, a barbecue was enjoyed by 3,500 people. (Courtesy of Florida Library and Archives, Florida Department of State.)

Chuck's Packaged Liquor Store was operated by Charles and Gertrude Huff. Almost 20 years since the repeal of Prohibition had softened the conservative views. It was an era of the cocktail, as popularized by movies, and a minimum drinking age was passed in the state. (Courtesy of Rick Moore.)

The Zephyrhills Golf Course was developed adjacent to the airport in the 1950s, and folks saw golf as a popular sport, no longer just a game for the idle rich. (Courtesy of ZHA.)

This Pierre Motel photograph was taken in 1978; the hosts were J. H. and Lucille Ramey, and it was located on North Highway 301. This was an era of family-owned motels and jazzy advertising, which included pool panoramas. (Courtesy of ZHA.)

Siesta Motel was operated by Dennis and Martha Desmond. It advertised breakfast, lunch, and dinner in a retro theme. (Courtesy of ZHA.)

Reutimann's second garage was a more well-known landmark and served as the Chevrolet dealership for many years. The former Amalie Waffler married Emil Reutimann in 1910, after which they came to the United States from Switzerland, settling in Tampa, where he worked as a machinist. In 1915, Zephyrhills was the next stop, with Emil setting up shop as an auto mechanic, which evolved into the Chevy dealership. (Courtesy of Wayne Reutimann.)

At Geiger's Lawn and Garden Supplies at 720 Seventh Street, one could purchase all the necessities of a garden—seedlings, onion sets, the works—as well as baby chicks and about any garden utensil. Always a hospitable location, it was also nice to visit a spell. It was sold in 2003. It was owned and operated by a descendant of the early settlers, Nathan Geiger. (Courtesy of ZHA.)

Eastman's Trailer Park's slogan was "Where Old Friend's Meet." (Courtesy of Rick Moore.)

Campers are recorded celebrating in 1953 at Winters' Park. "The tourist industry has been good to us," said Helen Winters, wife of the late Gordon Winters, who owned Winters' Park. It is the oldest mobile home park in town. "In 1962 for most of our people that came from the north, the park was their sole source of activity. We had 16 shuffleboard courts and we had to limit people to 3 games at a time. They were more like a big family at that time." (Courtesy of ZHA.)

A picnic at Winters' Park in 1953 was a sumptuous feast. The park is operated by Bob Winters and his wife, Christine, in 2009. (Courtesy of ZHA.)

The 1957 varsity basketball starters were, from left to right, Larry Hill, David Bright, David Fedor, Paul Canaday, and Steve Huber. The town was known for its basketball dynasty of the 1960s. From 1960 to 1966, Zephyrhills reached the Class B (equivalent to today's 2A) state tournament every season except one, with championships in 1961–1962 and 1963–1964. (Courtesy of ZHS.)

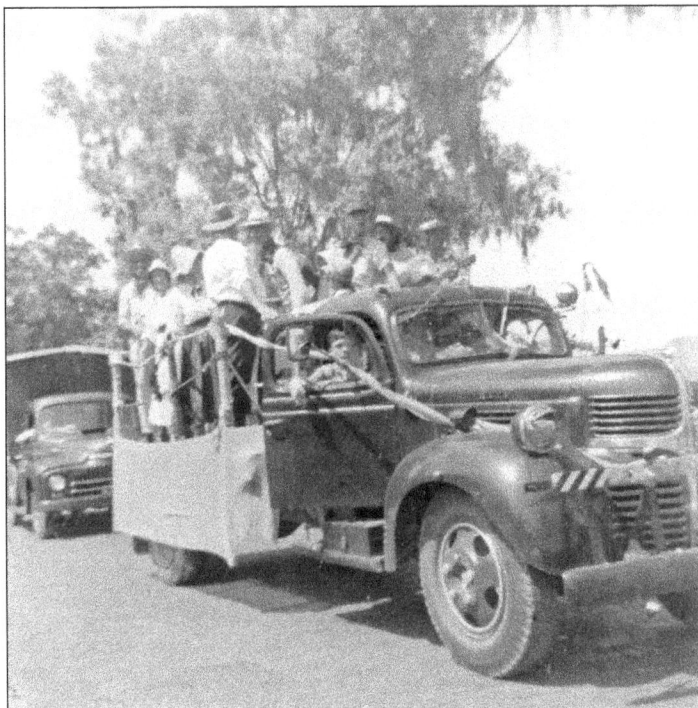

The 1953 Founder's Day Parade reflected the "happy days" era. The school play included *Little Miss Spitfire* starring George Neukom, Helen Wells, H. C. Nesbit, and Joan Lefler, and *Deadly Earnest* starring Lamar Massey, Vonceil Clardy, Carol Sibley, and Margaret Seppanen. (Courtesy of ZHA.)

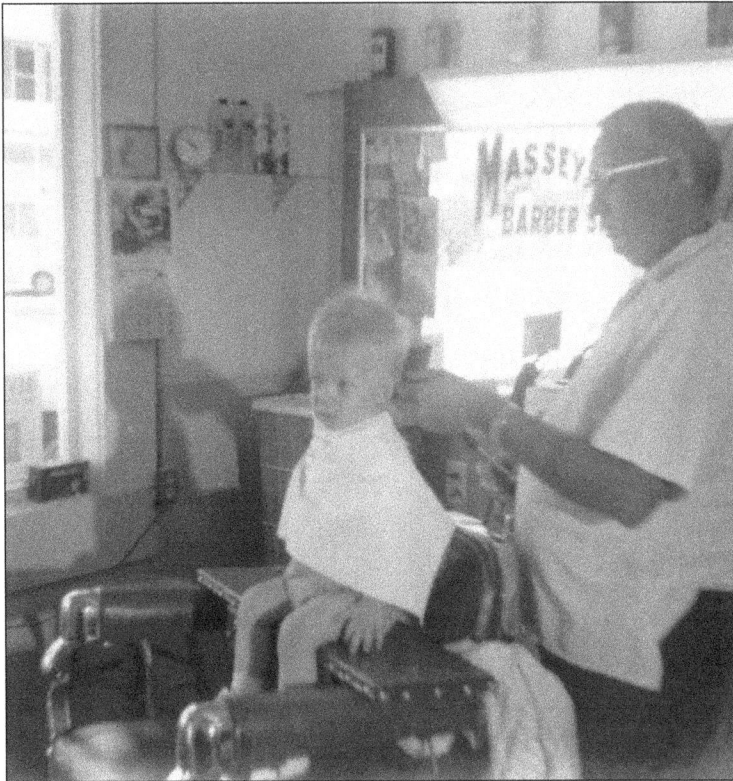

Massey's Barber Shop is one of the oldest shops in Zephyrhills. Bud Massey operated the shop from 1948 to 1992. In 1952, haircuts were 65¢ and a shave was 35¢. This photograph shows Bud Massey giving a first haircut to Paul McHenry Jr. "The shop was kind of like a step back into time . . . antique shaving cups, mugs, fireplace and spittoon. They solve all the world problems right there in the shop," said the *News*. (Courtesy of Nancy Perkins.)

In the mid-1950s, research showed that Americans were spending less on books and more on radios, televisions, and musical instruments. Betty Hall and Celia Anderson were leaders in encouraging people to read in Zephyrhills at the National Library Week event. (Courtesy of ZHS.)

The community barbecue for Founder's Day 1988 included, from left to right, Jim Childres, chamber of commerce president John Knowles, Jerry Burgess, and Carlton Galster at Zephyr Park. (Courtesy of ZHA.)

The local icehouse, Kerr's Cold Storage, was operated by James and Geraldine Kerr. "I began working in the afternoons and on Saturdays during high school, but worked there until the business, which had opened on October 1, 1944, closed on October 1, 1969," said Wayne Bodiford. "The location was beside and nearly under the original water tower—downtown, and it had wooden butcher blocks, sawdust floors and a wood-fired Smokehouse." (Courtesy of Margaret Nelson Cherry.)

Captain Jeffries's house, here in the 1910s, has continued as a community symbol throughout the town's history. (Courtesy of ZHA.)

Robert K. Napier, a pharmacist who was previously connected with City Drug Store, opened Napier Drug Store in 1933. He rented the Garside building on Seventh Street East opposite the Tourist Club. (Courtesy of ZHA.)

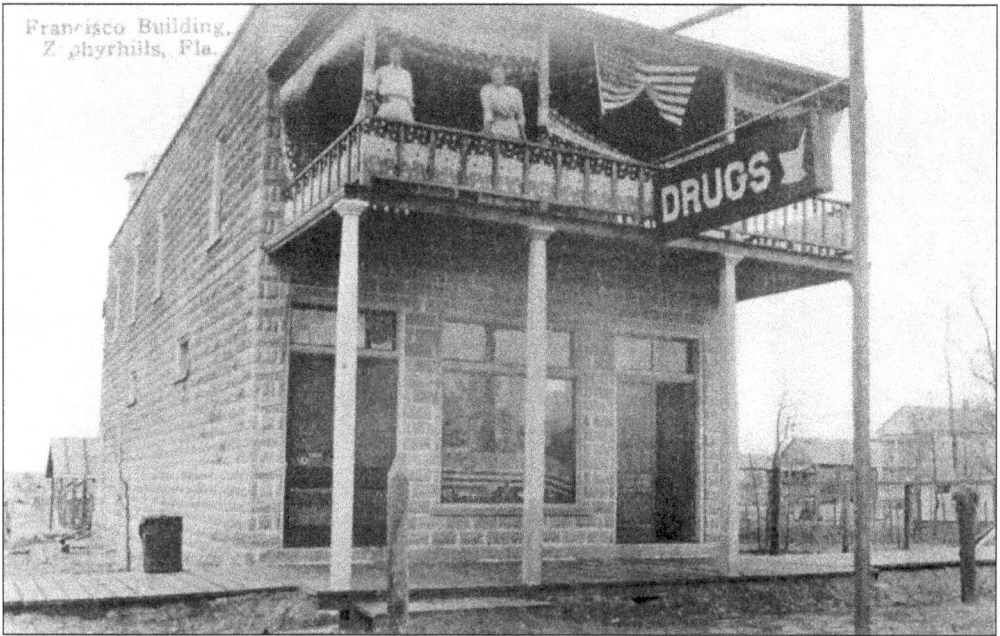

The first block structure was built in 1911 by Waldo M. Francisco. Francisco was an innovator in early Zephyrhills. He was the first to have electricity and developed the first electric power plant, which evolved into Zephyrhills Electric Company. (Courtesy of ZHA.)

The Miller children are pictured in front of the local drugstore, which posted a sign announcing "War Bond Sales." The photograph, taken in 1945, shows, from left to right, Larry, Glenn, Nancy, and Craig Miller enjoying a refreshing ice cream cone in downtown Zephyrhills. One can feel the hometown warmth. (Courtesy of ZHA.)

This image of a crank automobile with Helen Miller is in the vintage photograph collection at the Zepyrhills Depot Museum. (Courtesy of ZHA.)

Crystal Springs was a recreational location throughout its entire history. This photograph from a private family collection showed the springs before a dam was built, which altered its appearance. (Courtesy of Vicki Kingston.)

The 1952 prom was hosted in the VFW building. Everyone posed in their gowns and suits for the annual photograph. (Courtesy of M. Massey.)

Zephyrhills's African American students attended a local school (one room at the Krusen Quarters) but later were bused to the Dade City Moore Academy (named after J. D. Moore, an early teacher). The African American school at Krusen Quarters in Zephyrhills had two teachers: Bessie Barefield, who also served as principal, and Martha L. Lewis. (Courtesy of ZHA.)

One of the earliest homes in Zephyrhills was at 619 Tenth Street at the southwest corner of Seventh Avenue. It was occupied over time by the S. P. Boyer family, then Dr. and Mrs. Lamb, and later Eve Sanders. (Courtesy of ZHA.)

Boy Scouts have been a service group in Zephyrhills for many years. Jeff Travis contributed that his father, Bob Travis, was the Cubmaster of Pack 403. The Robert and Terry Hilferding family, with adult sons Eric and Gregg, have a long history of leadership in the community. This troop was later known as the "Eagle Troop," because they achieved many Eagle ranks. The 1950s troop was on a Scout excursion to Dade Battlefield in nearby Sumter County, a park that commemorates the Seminole resistance to forced removal in 1835 by Maj. Francis Dade, an act which prompted the Second Seminole War. The troop leaders were Floyd Kingston and Lee Reed, and Scouts in the photograph are, from left to right, (first row) Mike Lane; (second row) Gary Bracknell, Dean Martinson, Larry Chancey, Dick Dibble, and Dale Anderson; (third row) David Grant, Larry Turner, Marvin Reed, and Frank Overhuls; (fourth row) Tommy Ross, Curtis Crist, Glen Ehlers, Bob Winters, Allen Ward, Jed Wilkinson, Russell Kirk, Chuckie Johnson, Harry Mortner, David Kaylor, Reggie Brown, Sam Surratt, Sam Taylor, Eddie Strube, Westfall Uterhardt, Dexter Uterhardt, and Mark Higginson. (Courtesy of Vicki Kingston.)

Five

TAKE A LOOK

Merriel Miller Dancers performed for many years in the Zephyrhills area as an offshoot of the Tourist Club. They kicked up their heels in period costumes and were accomplished at square dancing and ballroom dancing. The leader was Helen Miller. (Courtesy of ZHA.)

Walter R. Gall was originally from Indiana and was instrumental as a realtor, entrepreneur, and civic leader. He purchased 30,000 acres for $3 per acre in the early 1920s (including land that now encompasses Saddlebrook Resort). His residence, shown here, was used for various businesses as well as his home. (Courtesy of ZHA.)

An aerial view in 1962 shows Sibley's Lumber Company in the front middle. The lumber company is now the site of SunTrust Bank on Gall Boulevard. Just to the right of the domed buildings was by Chenkins Packing. Herman and Rose Chenkins established Chenkins Packing (later known as Natural Foods Company, Inc., in 1924) and operated it until 1966. The building at the front right was Tyson General Store. (Courtesy of Clereen Morrill Brunty.)

Constance Kaylor was a teacher in the community schools for nearly 40 years. She and her husband, Jesse Kaylor, operated an area business, Kaylor Hardware. Quite the women's rights advocate, she campaigned with the school board and won the right for female teachers to hold their jobs while expecting children, a practice that was not endorsed in the early 20th century. (Courtesy of ZHS.)

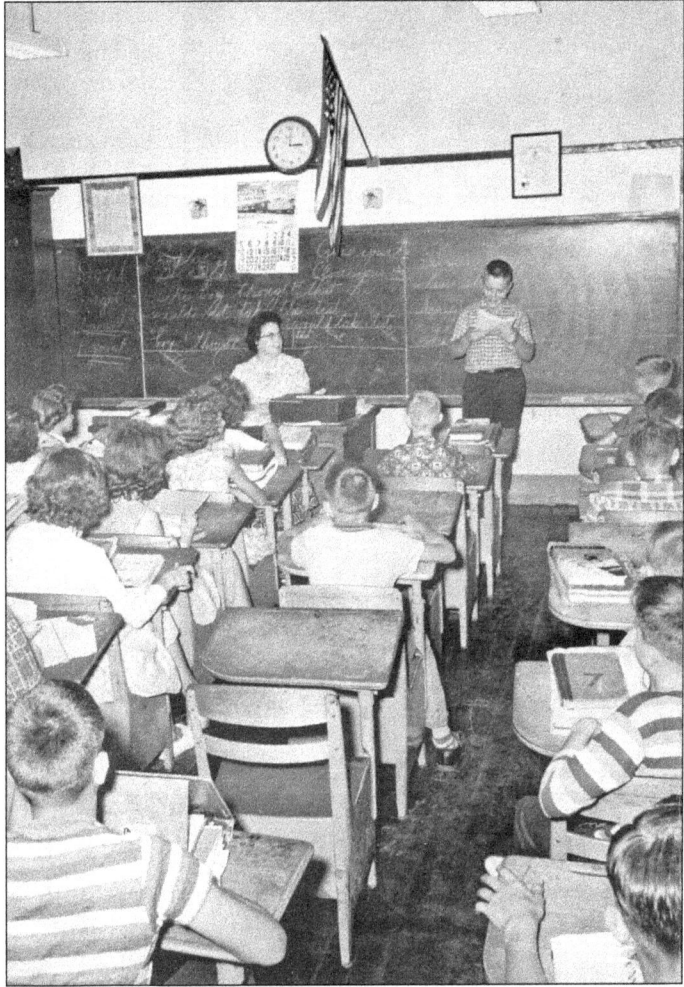

This aerial view of Zephyrhills by Wayman's Studio confirmed the rural nature of the day—wide-open spaces. (Courtesy of Rick Moore.)

Aerial view Zephyrhills. Fla.
looking E

Zephyrhills Photo Series.
Wayman's Studio.

In 1952, Kentucky dairy farmer Jack Linville and his wife, Lois, came to Zephyrhills to develop what was to become the biggest single business for many years, Zephyr Egg Company. "We started off with 500 chickens and we have more than 2 million now," said Danny Linville, Jack's son and Zephyr Egg's general manager until it was sold a few years ago. "Jack Linville's strength," Danny said, "was in running his own feed mill, from which he marketed feed to all the neighboring counties." (Courtesy of Nick Linville.)

The school auditorium in 1963 was a major meeting location and hosted the orientation meeting for a new school year. When the building was demolished to make way for a modern site in 2005, stories of class plays, graduations, and ceremonies of all types were revisited by locals. (Courtesy of ZHS.)

Zephyr Hills School, Zephyr Hills, Fla.

The third school building was reconstructed with the help of Roosevelt's WPA project and opened once again in 1937 with great pride at Tenth Avenue and Tenth Street. Student Ronald Springfield wrote, "Sandhill cranes flying over head, but not seen. / Friends talking, but not heard. / A rose within reach but the fragrance is not enjoyed. / Life itself, thinking there will always be tomorrow." (Courtesy of Rick Moore.)

Celery Farm, Zephyrhills, Fla.

There was a need for more alternative vegetable crops after the freeze of 1894 impacted the citrus crop. Celery was attempted for several years in the Zephyrhills area and was shipped in barrels. (Courtesy of ZHA.)

The original "00" car was photographed with pride by a local race car fan. Legend has it that Boobie Reutimann showed his latest hot rod to his father, Emil, who said, "That car is the nearest to nothing I've seen. . . . I'd call it a double nothing!" Thus the Reutimann brand began. (Courtesy of Norman Blackburn.)

School cafeteria staff in 1957 included, from left to right, Vera Holt, Lois Stewart, Jean Sellers, Louise Taylor, Bertie Bird, Sylvia Geiger, Rose Allen, and Elizabeth Mathis. (Courtesy of ZHS.)

Six

PRECIOUS ARTIFACTS

Cemetery Fountain was built in 1939. Abram Elias Geiger and his wife, Sarah, homesteaded 160 acres west of Zephyrhills. Geiger Cemetery was on part of what was this original Geiger property. Abram Geiger's family moved to the Plant City area about 1860. Abram, at the age of 15, joined the same Florida company in the Civil War to which his father belonged. (Courtesy of Rick Moore.)

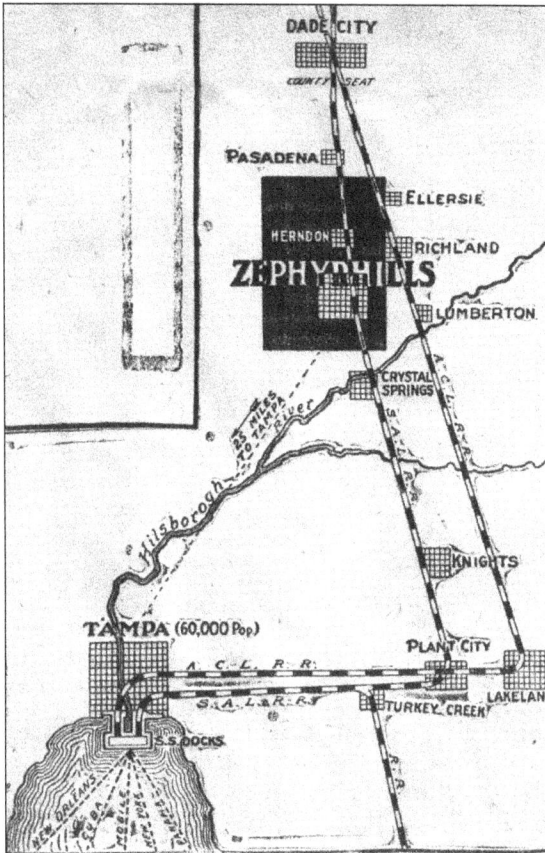

This 1957 parade featured an exhibit from the Zephyrhills Garden Club. The Garden Gate Circle tree project from the Zephyrhills Garden Club facilitated the naming of Zephyrhills as a "Tree City" in 2002. Raybelle Surratt was instrumental in developing a tree memorial dedication planting program that planted more than 700 trees in the city, each with a story. "Every piece of property owned by the city—we've planted a tree on it," said Surratt, "including trees for fallen soldiers and 'Mayor's Row.' These Are Amazing Women and a club that evolved from flower arranging to community activism." (Courtesy of Vicki Kingston.)

A vintage map of Zephyrhills dated October 5, 1911, was hand-drawn and showed the names of nearby towns Herndon and Ellerslie (misspelled on the map) as well as the path of the Hillsborough River (also misspelled). It noted that the 1911 population of Tampa of 60,000. The map portrayed the paths from the docks in Tampa with mention of Cuba, New York, and elsewhere in a novel fashion. (Courtesy of ZHA.)

From the March 1914 Official Directory of Zephyrhills and Colony printed by Floyd A. Gibson was a page that proclaimed, "The Colony that made good—The land of Flowers and Cool Breezes." As a caption to the picture, it invited the viewer to take a "birds eye view," looking east from the Hennington Block. It concluded with "Why not come to Zephyrhills?" (Courtesy of ZHA.)

An advertisement on the postcard lists key facts: 1) Established January 2, 1910; 2) First house built February 1910 as well as 23 establishments, which notably included a telephone exchange, 6 teachers and 200 pupils, and electric light plant. It boasted the "main line of Seaboard Railroad and 4 passengers stops daily." The quote appealed to potential pioneers as it proclaimed, "Any good industrious man can make a good living for a family on 10 acres of this land." (Courtesy of ZHA.)

ZEPHYRHILLS, FLORIDA
"The Colony That Made Good"
The land of Flowers and Cool Breezes

Birds Eye View Looking East from The Tennington Block

The above is a picture showing a portion of Fifth Avenue taken a few months ago. Three years ago a picture taken from this same place would have shown nothing but a railroad, trees and grass. Your attention is called to Fifth avenue which crosses the Railroad and is a 90 foot thoroughfare. Seventh Street which runs with the railroad is 60 foot on each side of the right of way which is two hundred feet. This gives wide streets in the business part of town thereby preventing congestion of traffic as the town grows. Zephyrhills is not a place to remain a small town but is destined to be one of the best inland cities in south Florida. It has a country to back it and is being settled with a progressive people to make it. Why not come to Zephyrhills.

Griffins Drug Co. Inc.   Dade City.   Jewelry and Silverware

THEZEPHYRHILLS COLONY WAS ESTABLISHED JANUARY 1st, 1910
The first house was built in February of the same year. We have grown until now we have a population of about 2000.

WE HAVE

1 Department Store	1 Drug Store	Good Public School Graded
4 General Mdse. Stores	1 Livery Stable	6 Teachers, 200 Pupils
3 Grocery Store	1 Blacksmith Shop	3 Churches
4 Hotels and Restaurants	2 Shoe Shops	Weekly Newspaper
1 Meat Market	1 Jewelry Store	Telephone Exchange
1 Barber Shop	1 Jewelers Shop	Bakery
2 Hardware Stores	1 Furniture Store	Electric Light Plant
	2 Ice Cream Parlors	State Bank

We are on the main line of Seaboard Railroad and have 4 passenger trains daily. Land is high and rolling, some quite hilly, some of these hills attain the hight of over 200 feet. Our land is fertile and produces everything that is produced in the state. Soil is a sandy loam mixed with clay. Water very best, free from mineral or other disagreeable substances. Our water bearing rock is quartz. The health is the best. No malaria or other fevers. Any good industrious man can make a good living for a family on ten acres of this land.

WHAT WE NEED

A Good Water Works System, a Good Ice Plant, and a Good First Class Hotel.

A vintage postcard postmarked August 1918 was sent to Cimarron, Kansas, and had an array of photographs, which included Seventh Street, Fifth Avenue, and the public school. A 2¢ stamp has also been cancelled out. (Courtesy of Rick Moore.)

ZEPHYRHILLS COLONY
COMPANY

was incorporated in 1909 and purchased the site for Zephyrhills Colony. This land was laid off into 5-acre tracts with one section in town lots which is the town of Zephyrhills. We have spent thousands of dollars in advertising, opening up streets, roads, making roads etc. Our company is far different from the large per cent of land development companies operating in Florida. This company is here not only to sell land, but to continue to improve Zephyrhills and make it one of the best inland towns in the country. We know that we have the natural resources and advantages and we are here to stay, all the officers of the company having their homes here

We have quite a large amount of land yet and buying more all the time. We have land in all parts of the Colony as well as lots in all parts of the town. We take pleasure in showing our property as well as giving any desired information by mail. We have had many years experience in Florida with citrus fruits and vegetables and are ready and willing to advise you.

ZEPHYRHILLS COLONY
COMPANY, Inc.
Office Near Depot

Pasco County Hardware & Supply Co. Crockery, Glassware

Encapsulated into a number 1, this advertisement of 1914 cleverly appealed to those interested in settling in Zephyrhills. It boasted about the natural resources and mentioned that the Zephyrhills Colony Company was very accessible and near the depot. (Courtesy of ZHA.)

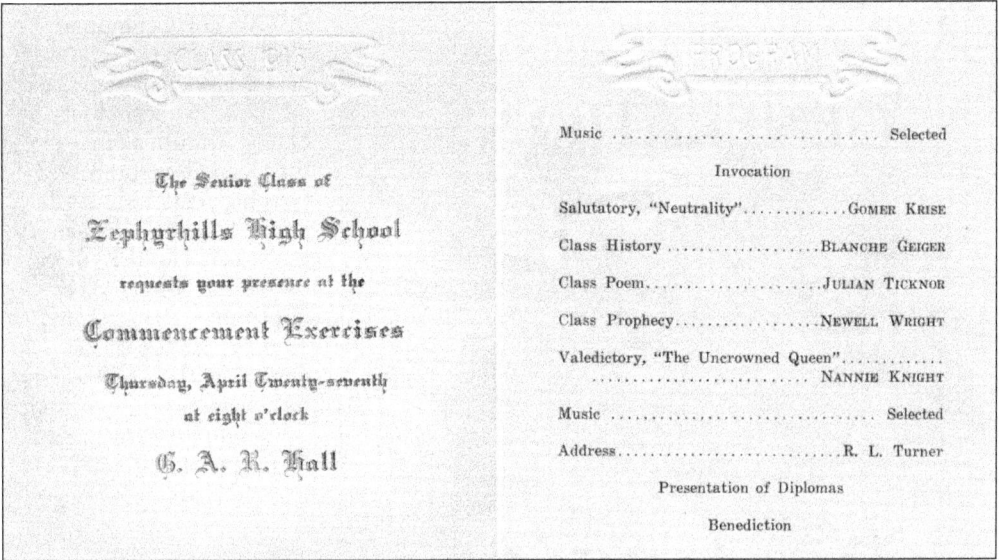

The Senior Class of

Zephyrhills High School

requests your presence at the

Commencement Exercises

Thursday, April Twenty-seventh

at eight o'clock

G. A. R. Hall

Music	Selected
Invocation	
Salutatory, "Neutrality"	GOMER KRISE
Class History	BLANCHE GEIGER
Class Poem	JULIAN TICKNOR
Class Prophecy	NEWELL WRIGHT
Valedictory, "The Uncrowned Queen"	NANNIE KNIGHT
Music	Selected
Address	R. L. Turner
Presentation of Diplomas	
Benediction	

An embossed 1916 graduation invitation, which was tied in green woven string, announced the April 27, 1916, graduation ceremony and its surrounding events. The five graduates of the town's only school were Julian Ticknor, Nanie Knight, Newell Wright, S. Blanche Geiger, and W. Gomer Krise. Their class motto was "To Thine Own Self Be True." (Courtesy of ZHS.)

Could there have been sex appeal in early Zephyrhills? This 1914 postcard would certainly indicate such. The postcard is in the colors of bright orange and beige and the wording says, "Cherries are always ripe in Zephyr Hills. Get in the Game—it's great!" The image is a couple in an intense embrace hidden behind an umbrella. The postcard from Rick Moore's collection was postmarked April 20, 1914, and was written by "Belle" to Wallace Cooper in Gulfport, Florida. In the narrative, she wrote, "Mama and Papa have gone to see Aunt Nellie and Jim Kersey. Lawrence has gone to Geigers to see his girl and Flora and I are at home." The 1¢ postage stamp rounded out the vintage feel of the artifact. (Courtesy of Rick Moore.)

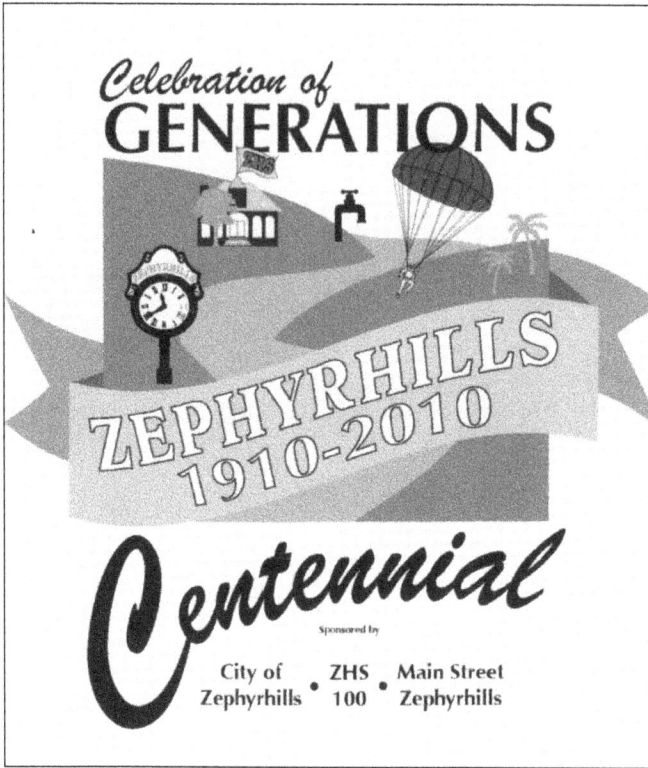

In 2008, the Centennial Committee of the school held a development contest for the school logo. Mary Lee Going Griffith, alumni of the local school from 1993 (graphic artist and Florida State University graduate), was selected for the school centennial posters to be displayed at Homecoming 2010. Notice the classic symbols of the town: water, parachute, first school, and community cohesiveness. (Courtesy of ZHS.)

The Zephyrhills Water Tower was erected in 1923 on Seventh Street. It replaced a previous wooden tower and stood 172 feet high. It was torn down in 1985. (Courtesy of WPHS.)

Seven

PARTING GLIMPSES

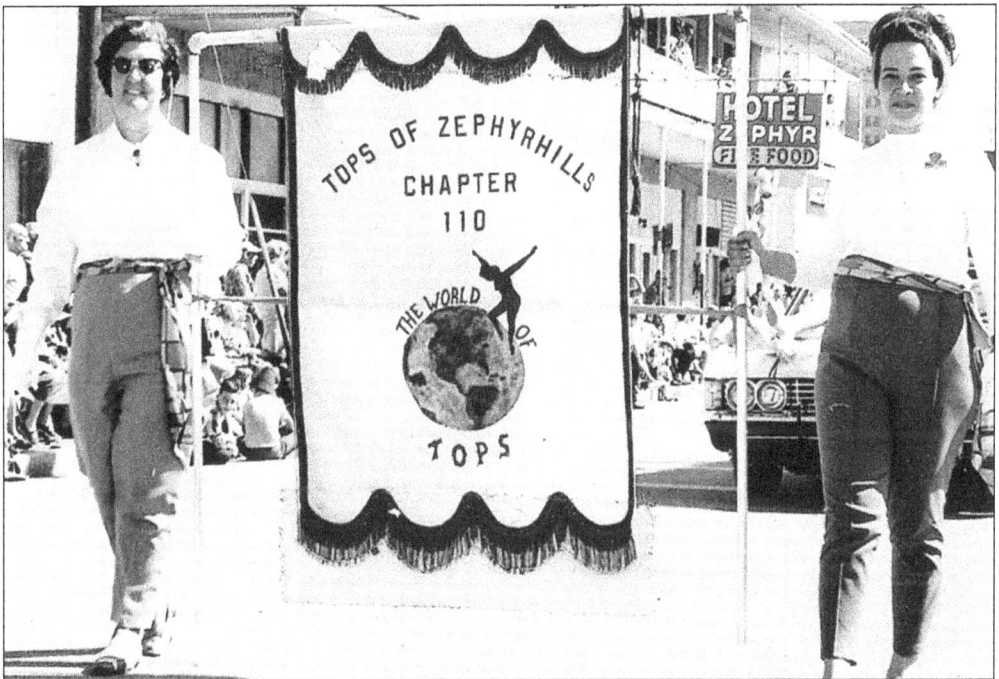

Mary Warder (left) and Kay Garland marched in the TOPS (Take Off Pounds Sensibly) unit in the 1960 parade in downtown Zephyrhills. Hurricane Donna impacted the community in September 1960; the local school was used as a hurricane shelter, and the school principal, Dr. Charles Henderson, remembered that he had to venture out in his 1950 Ford in the midst of the storm to fetch Dr. B. G. Wilkinson to attend to the three pregnant ladies in the shelter. (Courtesy of Kay Garland.)

Here is Zephyrhills in the 1960s—a downtown look. The post–World War II era brought the introduction of air-conditioning and the interstate highway, which encouraged renewed migration from the North. Due to low tax rates and a warm climate, Zephyrhills, just north of Tampa, became a destination for many retirees from the Northeast, Midwest, and Canada. (Courtesy of ZHA.)

The 1960 Journalism Club at the local high school divulged the changes in technology over the years. A hand-crank mimeograph machine was high-tech in those days. Folks included, from left to right, Libby Jarrett, teacher Alpha Gill, Vivian Geiger, and Margaret Johnson. (Courtesy of ZHS.)

116

The Ways and Means Committee of the Garden Club brought the Doris Gorrecht concert on March 2, 1951, at the Home Theatre. Gorrecht provided a harp concert. The theater was used for commencements and community presentations throughout the 1950s. Its predecessor was the Zephyrhills Theatre. (Courtesy of ZHA.)

The First family (Mary Crawford First with sons Gary at left and Greg) traveled to Cleveland, Ohio, to visit the boys' grandmother in 1960. They boarded the train at the depot where the Village Inn is now located. "At that age, nothing was more fun than riding a train, especially visiting the dining car," said Greg, who has been the "voice of the local school" for over 20 years as the sports announcer. (Courtesy of ZHA.)

The local yearbook chronicle, *Zephilsco*, was named in 1948 by Jane Kerr and her mother, Geraldine Kerr, and Jane's classmate Betty Jo Turner. *Zephilsco* staff in 1951 included Rex Gilreath, Mary Ann Vestal, Nelda Rae Cook, Joyce Baker, Jack Lamb, Bill Stallings, Marilyn McClellan, Barbara Sabin, Donald Welsch, Cynthia Hinsz, Helene Rexroad, and Martha Mae Keller. The 1951 class history reads: "Our trip on Easter Sunday to the Singing Tower was very enjoyable and one not forgotten easily. . . . Days have come and gone and with them are many memories." (Courtesy of ZHS.)

The girls' physical education building in 1965 showed the use of a building that previously housed the hot lunch program. (Courtesy of ZHS.)

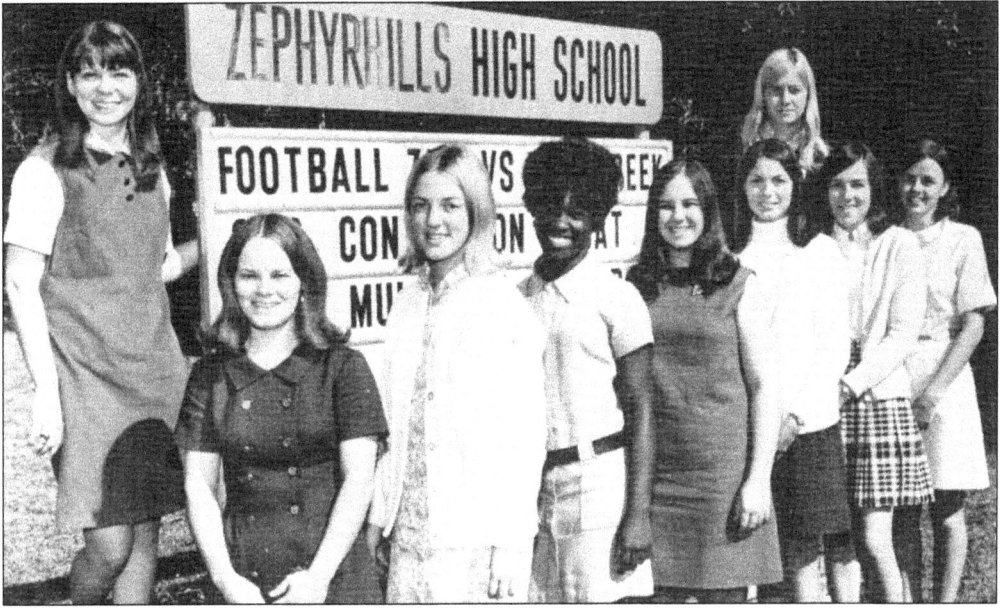

A sign announced the local school in the 1960s. This was the era of the first development of the so-called I-4 Corridor—an interstate linking Tampa, Lakeland, Orlando, and Daytona Beach—which was popularized in the early elections of the 21st century because of population size and potential swing votes. A 1970s Civinette group (a local citizenship and community service organization for teens) poses in front of the school. From left to right are Irene Graf, Joyce Emery, Debbie Simmons, Mae Alice McKenzie, Donna Darby, Nancy Walker, Anne Phipps, Beverly Carroll, and Pat Artabasy. (Courtesy of ZHS.)

The *Colonist* (also known as the *Pasco Free Press* and *Zephyrhills News*) has been published since 1911. The first proprietors of the *News* were George H. Gibson, editor, and Floyd A. Gibson, foreman. The paper was originally published in Tampa. In 1914, an advertisement said, "For $1 per year (paid in advance), one could have the weekly." The most well-known editor was Bernie Wickstrom. (Courtesy of ZHA and Margaret Seppanen.)

Pictured is the classroom of Helen Hamilton at Zephyrhills School. Esther Austin McGavern wrote, "The classroom seemed warm and inviting; now I would think of it as sweltering. It had big open windows, high ceilings, and a picture of George Washington and an old master's art print. Helen Hamilton decorated her room with seasonal crepe paper blackboard borders printed by the Dennison Paper Company. To me, they were just wonderful. Now, vintage Dennison paper holiday decorations are highly collectible." (Courtesy of ZHS.)

This 1950s-era shot shows the establishments of Sibley's, Senn's 5-and-10, and the local theater. (Courtesy of Vicki Kingston.)

In the 1950s, the Zephyrhills downtown was still the vital center for community members for shopping and congregating. Developers had begun in the 1950s to build inexpensive houses that attracted retirees and began development that is still seen in the 21st century. (Courtesy of Pioneer Museum.)

Coach John Clements and his wife, Beanie, were given a mural-size photograph of his debut as grand marshal in the 2007 Founder's Day Parade. This was presented at the 2007 Community Alumni Picnic and has been signed by all present. Clements organized the first Little League in 1952. (Courtesy of Clereen Morrill Brunty.)

The 1979 highlight event was the unveiling of the football stadium. A plaque affixed to the stadium contains a list of contributing contractors, memoriam, committee members, and actual contributors. The Quarterback Club/Bulldog Boosters were instrumental, and the fund-raising effort was the largest in the community until the FHZ Heart Beat 2000 for the hospital, which opened in 1984. (Courtesy of Ernest Wise.)

Students are shown in front of the school in 1926. This decade was a practical one. The class of 1928's motto was "Onward ever," and the class of 1926's was "Labor has a sure reward." The newspaper accounts reported that the students hauled clay for their baseball field in 1927. Sports during the decade were local events or contests between informal groups. The weekly school events included a chapel service. Pageants and recitations were common at Thanksgiving and other holidays. (Courtesy of Elizabeth Geiger.)

The barracks were first used by the 10th Fighter Squadron in 1943–1944 at the Zephyrhills Airport. They have been used by the local fire department, various business enterprises, and as a temporary public school facility during a population boom in the mid-1940s. As seen driving by the airport, they are still utilized in 2009. (Courtesy of Ernest Wise.)

The enormous oaks mark the area and offer local charm. (Courtesy of ZHA.)

Ernie and Madonna Wise served as grand marshals of the founding event in 2009. Ernie was a media specialist/teacher for 35 years in the local high school, and Madonna was a community principal and author. The girls behind the car are Rachel Wise (left) and Sarah Touchton. (Courtesy of Clereen Morrill Brunty.)

T. K. Hayes, coordinator of Sky Dive City in Zephyrhills, operates a world-class parachute center. Since the late 1960s, skydivers from all over the world compete in "boogies," which included the Thanksgiving Boogie, Easter Boogie, and World Record Dives. He says, "We'll have divers come from as a far as Romania. . . . There should be up to 8,000 jumps in the week leading up to New Year's." (Courtesy of T. K. Hayes.)

"Skydive City" is a moniker for the area. On almost any day, the sky near the airport facility will be dotted with colorful parachutes, some boasting the city's name. (Courtesy of T. K. Hayes.)

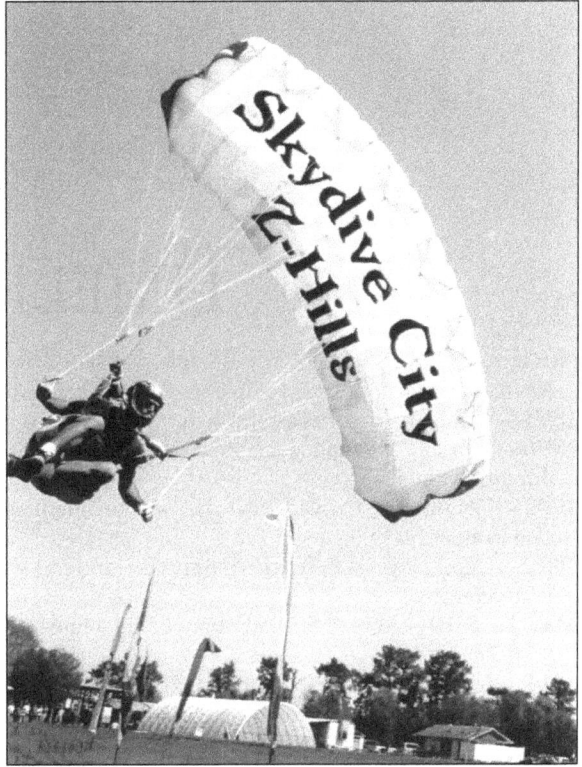

Let's have a final cheer for good old Zephyrhills from the 1960 school cheerleaders. They reflect the spirit of the town and the sense of community that has developed throughout time. The photograph features, from left to right, Brenda Howell, Virginia Hinsz, Lola Padgett, Alice Bembry, Melissa Lippincott, and Marion Canaday. (Courtesy of ZHS.)

TIMELINE

NOVEMBER 11, 1886—Simon J. Temple purchased 280 acres of land from Florida Railway and Navigation Corporation. Temple named the area Abbott after Dr. Joseph M. Abbott.

1893—Voting district was established.

1896—"Station" was added to name when the Seaboard Coast Line Depot was built to handle shipping of lumber.

1902—Community thrived with the establishment of First Baptist Church and Hennington's Department Store.

1909—Capt. Howard B. Jeffries purchased land in December 1909 to initiate a colony for Civil War veterans.

MAY 31, 1910—Abbott Station changed its name to Zephyrhills via the naming of the official post office.

1914—Zephyrhills was incorporated.

1920s–1930s—Farming remained the base of the local economy. "There was a cotton gin, turpentine still and tobacco barn," said Owen Gall in 1922.

1930s—Depression. The Florida land boom busted in 1927–1928, and it hit Zephyrhills hard. The only bank in town closed, as did the main local industry, Greer's Lumber Mill on Wire Road.

1932—I. A. Krusen moved to Zephyrhills and purchased 13,000 acres, which became Krusen Land and Timber Company.

1936—Highway 301 was built through Zephyrhills as a major link between East Pasco and Tampa.

1940s—New industry arrived in the form of the Hercules Powder Company, a firm that ground pine stumps and sent them to Brunswick, Georgia, to be processed into turpentine, rosin, and charcoal.

1942—Zephyrhills Municipal Airport was built as a training ground for the Army Air Force.

1947—The airport was deeded to Zephyrhills.

1950s—Tourism. This decade saw the beginning of tourism with a great influx of retirees. "When retired people came here, they could buy a real nice home for $7,500," said Fred Gill.

1952—Jack Linville came to Zephyrhills from Kentucky to found what was to become its biggest single business, Zephyr Egg Company. His unique feature was to operate his own feed mill, from which he marketed feed to neighboring counties.

1960s—Pasco began to receive an overflow of people from Hillsborough and Pinellas Counties.

1961—Don Robinson founded the Zephyrhills Water Company, which bottled water. The endeavor popularized the name of "Zephyrhills" throughout Florida and the Southeast.

1970s—Zephyrhills acquired its look of today: sprawling subdivisions of manufactured homes and mobile homes with restaurants and shopping plazas lining the main road and a population that nearly doubles in winter.

1984—East Pasco Medical Center (now Florida Hospital Zephyrhills) opened. The freezes of 1982 and 1983 damaged the citrus industry and made the economy more reliant on the service industry.

1990s—Zephyrhills continues as a retirement haven but has also become a bedroom community for Tampa as Wesley Chapel and New Tampa become closer.

BIBLIOGRAPHY

Anderson, Celia L. *The History of Education in Pasco County*. Dade City, FL: unfinished manuscript, 1980.

Dobson, Irene. Personal interview conducted by author. March 10, 2008.

Elkins, Vicki, and Margaret T. Seppanen. *Zephyrhills From A to Z*. Tampa, FL: The University of Tampa, 2008.

Falls, Carolyn. Consultation/Interview conducted by author at Pioneer Museum of Dade City/ Review of files in History Center at museum. February 11, 2008.

Florida Photographic Collection and Video Clips. State Library and Archives of the State of Florida, Florida Department of State, 2004. http://www.floridamemory.com (accessed January 1, 2009).

Horgan, James J., Alice F. Hall, and Edward J. Herrmann. *The Historic Places of Pasco County*. Vol. I. Dade City, FL: Pasco County Historical Preservation Committee, 1992.

Miller, Jeff, ed. "History of Pasco County–Zephyrhills." West Pasco Historical Society, 2002. http://www.fivay.org (accessed July 24, 2009).

Moore, Rick. Personal interview conducted by author in Zephyrhills. July 11, 2009.

Reeves, Victoria. Consultation conducted by author at Zephyrhills Depot. May 11, 2009.

Seppanen, Margaret. Personal interview conducted by author at Zephyrhills Depot. August 2, 2008.

Trottman, Rosemary W. *The History of Zephyrhills 1821–1921*. New York: Vantage, Inc., 1978.

Wise, Madonna J. *Tapestry: Zephyrhills: An Anthology of Its History Through Education*. Charleston, SC: Book Surge of USA, 2008.

www.arcadiapublishing.com

MAP SEARCH

Discover books about the town where you grew up, the cities where your friends and families live, the town where your parents met, or even that retirement spot you've been dreaming about. Our Web site provides history lovers with exclusive deals, advanced notification about new titles, e-mail alerts of author events, and much more.

MADE IN THE USA

Arcadia Publishing, the leading local history publisher in the United States, is committed to making history accessible and meaningful through publishing books that celebrate and preserve the heritage of America's people and places. Consistent with our mission to preserve history on a local level, this book was printed in South Carolina on American-made paper and manufactured entirely in the United States.

This book carries the accredited Forest Stewardship Council (FSC) label and is printed on 100 percent FSC-certified paper. Products carrying the FSC label are independently certified to assure consumers that they come from forests that are managed to meet the social, economic, and ecological needs of present and future generations.

FSC

Mixed Sources
Product group from well-managed forests and other controlled sources

Cert no. SW-COC-001530
www.fsc.org
© 1996 Forest Stewardship Council

Find Your Place in History.

www.ingramcontent.com/pod-product-compliance
Lightning Source LLC
Chambersburg PA
CBHW050614110426

42813CB00008B/2552